TRUE FREEDOM

A Revolutionary Approach
to Addiction Recovery

PART ONE

Escaping the Illusion

Rebekah S. Thomas

malcolm down
PUBLISHING

Endorsements

Reading through *True Freedom* made my heart leap with joy. It is extremely refreshing and revolutionary for recovery. Rebekah brings practical aids to our recovery and stories through which we can see our own lens emerge, providing a much needed pathway to journey out to lasting freedom.

I am convinced this new pathway for recovery will help any person struggling with addictive patterns of behaviour that can be hidden and cause repeated relapse. True Freedom brings what's hidden to the light where it can no longer have destructive power or influence in our lives. I highly recommend *True Freedom,* which can be run in a rehab or Church or one to one to heal a person's life.

Alison Fenning, RSVP Trust

In my 50+ years of ministry, I've worked with countless people who have been caught up in addiction. Bekah Thomas has written a fantastic guide that I believe will bring hope and purpose to many. *True Freedom* offers biblical, practical and incredibly wise counsel, which could be life transforming for many. She has not only provided great advice, but she has lived that advice, and in the book includes many examples of the lives she has seen changed. I pray this book will be a blessing to many.

Pastor Bill Wilson, Metro World Child.

Biblical, practical, clear and hopeful. This timely book will help many in their journey from addiction to freedom and I'm praying that it will be used widely and have a profound impact.

Gavin Calver, CEO, Evangelical Alliance.

The book is amazing. I LOVE it.

Like many other books this one deals with the science of addiction head on and how to break its destructive cycle. The psychology behind addiction is set out brilliantly. What makes this book unique, however, is that unapologetically it deals with recovery from addiction from a wholly Christian perspective. It sets out the hope of living free from its destruction, fear and self-loathing. It's realistic about the path of healing, outlining just how important the process is. Do you want to change? Do you know someone stuck in addition? Then read this book. I commend it highly.

Andrea Williams, Chief Executive, Christian Concern

I found Rebekah's take in *True Freedom* so refreshing and insightful. In many ways, a different angle from others, but one that works. I've seen this in the lives of many who pass through the Hope Centre.

Barry Woodward
Author of Once an Addict and CEO of Proclaim Trust

At the heart of all addiction is a pursuit. *True Freedom* is written with both passion and compassion. It is Spirit-led work that will bear much fruit. This is not a book to be read but a journey to engage with.

For many there is often a polarised choice between 12 steps or harm reduction, both of these - while proven and excellent often in practice – do not give a clarity to where truth and freedom is really found; this *True Freedom* work is abundantly clear.

Ian Mountford, Major
Corps Officer & Territorial Mission Enabler (THQ)*

I welcome this powerful and compelling book. Addiction robs people of their dignity and, ultimately, their destiny. From her experience helping people break free from life controlling addictions, Bekah offers in *True Freedom* a radical, hope filled and genuinely practical journey out of addiction into a new life of freedom and purpose.

Chris Cartwright, General Superintendent, Elim Penetecostal Churches.

I would consider Rebekah Thomas an expert on finding freedom from addiction, not just because of her personal story but also due to her many years of experience working with those who have struggled with addiction. I was so glad when I heard she took her years of experience and knowledge and put it into a book to help others. May this book encourage you, strengthen you, and help you to find true freedom.

Josh Hannah, Founder and President, Hope Center Ministries

True Freedom is a radical and carefully considered study, brought together through Rebekah's experience, learning and revelation. This is an exciting new approach that not only builds on former models but brings a new comprehensive dynamic to the understanding of what it means to experience and walk out True Freedom from addiction.

Trudy Makepeace, author, Abused. Addicted. Free.

Addiction is a curse that reaches beyond the user to affect everyone who feels its touch. What Rebekah has done is to map out a journey that, if followed, ends with release from the curse, and the start of a new journey of freedom. This really works – if you work it, and this book will benefit everyone who engages with it.

Rev. Paul Lloyd, Senior Pastor, Victory Outreach Manchester
VOI UK/Germany Regional Leader

I am honoured to recommend the *True Freedom* books by my friend, Rebekah Thomas. I have had the honour of seeing her work in Wales.

She lives out what she is teaching through this book. She pours her life into broken people day in and day out. Their organization is having a phenomenal impact on people on the pathway to freedom and healing.

Sujo John, Founder, YouCanFreeUs Foundation

First published 2022 by Malcolm Down Publishing Ltd.
www.malcolmdown.co.uk

25 24 23 22   7 6 5 4 3 2 1

British Library Cataloguing in Publication Data
A catalogue record for this book is available from the British Library.

ISBN 978-1-915046-39-0

Cover design by Angela Selfe

Printed in the UK

Disclaimer
This book is not a substitute for professional medical advice.
Readers are advised to see a GP if they are battling addiction.

Contents

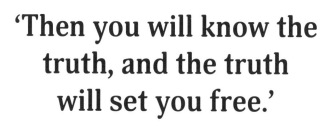

'Then you will know the truth, and the truth will set you free.'

John 8:32, the Bible

Introduction

I'm so excited that you've decided to take this journey with me. This book is the result of a long and gradual journey, during which God has opened my eyes to reveal deeper levels of truth through my experience, research, ever-evolving theology and prayer. I can't promise it will make your recovery easy (I'm not even sure that would be a good thing) or that it will set you free simply by reading the words on the page. But I can guarantee – based on my personal experience over the years of leading addicts into freedom – that if you are able to understand, apply and persist with the contents of this workbook you can live absolutely free of addiction, completely free from cravings and love life without the thing(s) that once controlled you.

I grew up around alcohol-fuelled chaos, violence, dysfunction and poverty. I went on to struggle with various addictions myself – even as a Christian who was deeply in love with Jesus and passionate about my discipleship after meeting him at the age of seven. My younger sisters have also struggled with addiction in various forms over the years. I later married a former crack and heroin addict, and have undertaken various roles within the addiction sector over the last fifteen years, as well as working in local church leadership and in secular teaching / training roles.

I can now say that all my own struggles with addiction were completely worth it to be able to share what God has taught me as a result. I used to wonder why he didn't just take my addictions away, as I'd seen him do for many others, but I now know that I needed to go through the experience to learn the things I did so I could share them with others.

For the last two-and-a-half years I've been leading a residential Christian addiction recovery programme, during which time I have taught the contents of this material. At first I primarily taught it at one of our centres because I was directly leading that centre at the time. But the women there insisted that I write it all down so the men at the other centres could learn what they had learned, so I did. Then I was encouraged to write it all down in a way that allowed others to benefit from it, and the workbook you are holding (along with the other True Freedom resources) is the result of that. At the end of this introduction are quotes from some of the recovering/former addicts in various stages of the True Freedom material who wanted to describe their experiences of using the book.

I want to honour the addiction recovery models that have gone before this one. They have great value in many ways. However, the True Freedom model is a new and valuable tool. This approach to addiction recovery works for addiction in general: from nicotine to crack; from sugar to opioids; from a life-destroying cycle of torture to something coming between you and a person or goal that matters.

It will work for you whether you're in a residential rehab that uses True Freedom, part of a local True Freedom Community group, in a prison reading True Freedom during a group session or from your cell, journeying through it at home after work each day, or if a mentor, loved one or chaplain / pastor / leader is supporting you through it on a one-to-one basis.

If you have no choice but to engage with these workbooks alone that's OK, but I would highly recommend seeking out a mentor to oversee your journey if that's an option. Look for someone who loves you enough to be honest, even if it doesn't make them popular. Someone who is insightful enough to empathise with your brokenness, and who is a faithful, fruitful disciple of Jesus.

If you get confused, ask that trusted person to help you. If you have unwanted thoughts and feelings, ask them to pray with you. If you struggle to read and write, or to focus, ask them to agree to a time and place to go through the workbook with you. True Freedom Community Groups will be available on the website, and you will be able to view supported housing options where True Freedom principles are taught.

The True Freedom journey begins with three separate parts of the True Freedom workbook. You are currently holding Part One, which unravels the deception that has kept you trapped, allowing you to move forward. Part Two unpacks the other forces at work in your life and in your addiction. Part Three leads us to take the action needed towards complete freedom from addiction.

Each milestone ends with a statement of truth, which can be read aloud as a declaration of your progress. At the end of all three parts, you will have twelve milestone statements you can remember as keys to freedom, all of which are recorded at the back of this book.

This workbook cannot take us everywhere I'd like to go because of space limitations. There is so much I can't or daren't cover here – details and rabbit holes that are worth thinking about but are either beyond my paygrade to publish, or are too vast, complex and tangential for the scope of this book.

As there are so many things there just isn't room for here, the True Freedom website (www.truefreedomrecovery. com) will include continually updated resources, including interview videos, additional illustrations, life-skills support, recommendations about other resources, leadership teaching, general discipleship, answers to your questions and prayer support. Mentors, loved ones, group leaders, chaplains and staff can also find what they need to support you and others to pursue true freedom through the website.

This book doesn't merely refer to God or have a Christian ethos; he is at the centre of every point, and it has only been written because of him. Having said that, I believe God is also at the centre of true science. Therefore, this book includes some material that is also promoted by non-Christians because it is so clearly true and so evidently works. As such, if Jesus Christ is not your Lord and Saviour, yet you have found yourself holding this book, there will still be plenty you can glean from it, and you will no doubt appreciate the content even if you dispute the source. There is an invitation to guided prayer at the end of every milestone, but there is no pressure to pray if you do not feel this is for you.

Many studies show that teaching others what we've learned is the best way to learn more deeply, so grab a journal, download a voice recorder app or make sure there's plenty of video space on your phone, because at certain points you'll see these images:

When you do, it's time to write, record or video yourself sharing what you've just learned in your own words, as if you're teaching it to someone else. If you have a mentor, friend or leader supporting you through this, read or play what you've recorded to them, and if you're part of a True Freedom group, share to teach each other what you've learned in your own words.

Much love,

Bekah

What other people are saying about True Freedom:

'It grips you before you realise it's about addiction, and then when the penny drops you're like, 'Wow, that's amazing!' It takes away the shame because now I know how addiction works.'
Debbie Greer

'When I started doing the milestones, it was like the author had been watching me; as if the milestones were tailor-made for me.'
Anthony Griffiths

'It's an outstanding piece of work, very interesting and insightful. Based on many years of addiction, I found this a simple and effective process, something I can carry into life.'
Mark Bailey

'Working through the True Freedom stuff is like finding the keys for a lock that no other place managed to help me find.'
Scott Warnock

'The milestones couldn't be more relevant. I thought I knew how things worked but I was wrong. I found the visual representation an eye-opener to what was actually happening to me.'
Craig Desmond

'When I picked up the workbook it blew me away – I thought it was aimed at me. This book will bring hope to others who are in despair.'
Charlotte Carradine

'This teaching helped me find true freedom from my addictions of alcohol and drugs of seventeen years. I tried other rehabs, counselling and recovery groups, and none of these worked for me. I am now actually living a life free from addiction, part of a local church community, marriage restored, running a Hope Centre and enjoying life free from addiction.'

Nicola Moseley (now employed in addiction recovery, using True Freedom material)

'I may have got clean without True Freedom, but I was not made well. True Freedom truly sets you free. It takes hold of so much recovery wisdom and becomes like a lens through which they make more sense.'

James Hackett (now employed in addiction recovery, using True Freedom material)

'It's just mind-blowing how you don't see it in the madness of living it, but True Freedom gives the light-bulb moment that sets you free.'

Lowri Marshall (now using the True Freedom material to lead addicts to the freedom she found)

Tom

Tom had just checked out and was heading out of the hotel lobby. He hadn't intended to stop, but he wasn't the kind of guy to shun a happy, loved-up couple. After all, who's too busy to take a photo for a couple of strangers? Well, he would have been back in the day, but he had since learned that life is better when you stop to smell the roses and help people. Achieving great success and accumulating enough wealth never to have to work another day unless he wanted to had certainly helped. He assumed that was why they had asked him; because he looked like a nice guy with enough time to stop and help. That and the fact he was standing nearby.

'Excuse me, sir,' the young woman had said, glowing.

She was just the right amount of bubbly. Enough to be charismatic, but not enough to be irritating.

'Would you mind?' She held out the camera the couple had been using to take selfies.

'Could you take our picture?' the young man clarified. He was also glowing, and he looked the friendly type.

Tom immediately liked them both. 'Yes, of course,' he responded, his voice automatically becoming as chirpy as theirs. He rested his suitcase on the ground beside him and placed his phone and coat on top of it to free up his hands. Then he took hold of the camera and waited for them to pose.

He took a couple of photos, then showed the couple, who fawned over each other. They twisted and turned in pursuit of better backdrops for the photos that would forever remind them of the morning after their first night as a married couple. Tom inched himself this way and that, attempting to capture the excited couple's ever-changing poses.

Feeling happy to have been able to share in and contribute to this lovely couple's special experience, Tom turned back to collect his belongings from the ground where he had laid them. But they were gone! There was an initial moment of confusion, then sheer panic set in. A few more glances around confirmed his fears. His bags had disappeared, along with his clothes, shoes, toiletries, laptop, tablet and wallet. Even his phone was gone.

The other guests and staff milling around became aware of Tom's panic, including the young newly-weds, who gasped as they realised what had happened. The moved in awkwardly, as if to help, but there was nothing they could do.

'My bags!' Tom exclaimed. Then, louder, 'My bags!' He could feel his pulse raising, his skin tingling. His body felt tight, as if it were somehow in his way.

More people moved towards him to offer help or to sympathise.

'Has anyone seen my bags?' he frantically asked the room.

'Here!' said a smartly dressed man, hurriedly handing Tom a phone. 'My sister's a detective. She'll sort you out . . . track your cards and so on. This is a direct line to her office.'

Tom pressed the man's phone to his ear, realising how hot his face had become. After two or three rings, a woman answered the phone.

'Hello?' she said, not recognising Tom's voice when he returned her greeting. 'Detective Inspector Bennet speaking.'

'Hello, Detective. My name's Tom. Your brother put me on to you because all my belongings have been stolen. My phone, my bank cards, everything!' He couldn't force his voice to stop shaking. He suddenly realised that panic was giving way to anger. Someone had taken his things. Someone had *stolen* them!

'OK, sir,' she said calmly. 'When did this happen?'

'Just now. It literally just happened, I . . . my stuff . . . ' he stammered. He looked down at the floor again, as if hoping his belongings would suddenly reappear and he could end the call.

'OK, that's good. We can track your phone and cards. We might even be lucky enough to get an image of the thief at a till or a cashpoint. I'm just going to need a few details from you.'

The calmness and authority in her voice made Tom feel calmer, and something suddenly switched inside him. He felt his muscles relax, even though he hadn't noticed them tensing up. His breathing slowed and he regained control of his voice. He breathed a deep sigh of relief, taking in the sounds of Detective Inspector Barratt's office in the background, feeling reassured that someone else was taking control.

Tom shared his details with the officer, giving her his address, date of birth, account details and everything else she needed to know. Then he hung up and thanked the helpful gentleman as he handed back the phone.

He looked around for the young couple but they had gone. He hadn't noticed them leave amid all the drama. He didn't blame them; it had hardly been a celebration-friendly incident.

What Tom didn't know was that the young couple, the man with the phone and the woman at the other end of the phone were all working together to not only steal his property, but to obtain the personal details they needed to access his accounts electronically. The couple – who weren't really a couple at all – had faked being newly-weds by highlighting their wedding ring fingers and fawning all over each other, pretending to care about backdrops so they could subtly coax Tom into turning his back on his luggage. They hadn't been able to believe their luck when he put his phone and pricey coat down on top of his case.

With his back turned, an inconspicuous woman had casually swooped in behind Tom, picking up everything he had been carrying and calmly walking out of the hotel lobby. The same lady had loaded Tom's things into her van, then jumped into the passenger seat and turned on the sound system, which had been preset to play office sounds. Within seconds, her phone had rung. She had taken the call, pretending to be Detective Inspector Barratt, and noted down all of Tom's details, reassuring him that he could relax and trust her to prioritise his case. Then she had hung up with a smile on her face.

Moments later, another member of the team – the 'brother' – had opened the driver's door and got in. Having waited nearby for a while, the young 'couple' had joined them and they had calmly driven away.

Worst of all, Tom was under the impression that his phone was being tracked by the police, so he didn't report or try to track it himself. He also believed his accounts were being tracked and would be blocked, giving the con artists time to take all his money and sell his property long before he was able to check his accounts. What a mess!

Milestone One:

Understanding That
Addiction Is a Trick

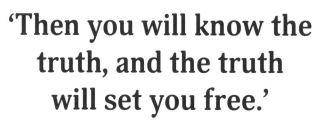

'Then you will know the
truth, and the truth
will set you free.'

John 8:32

It's a Trick

I saw the con involving Tom in an episode of a reality show called *Hustle*. In it, a team of very clever people aimed to help the general public avoid scams like this by showing how various hustles worked. The premise was that people wouldn't fall for a trick they understood.

Knowing how a trick works makes you less likely to be taken in by it again. If you come up against a simple magic trick in which the magician takes £10 from you each time you fall for it, you will quickly learn how it was done and avoid falling for it again. But when it's a more complex, cleverer trick like the one described above, it might not be so easy to avoid. You'd be less likely to fall for it once you knew how it worked, but there is still no guarantee. Tom could potentially fall for that con a second time if a different group of hustlers used a similar setup, but he wouldn't fall for it time and time again. The best chance a person has to avoid falling for a scam of this calibre is to study and really understand how it was done.

It's one thing to receive information, but the *knowing* of truth that Jesus talks about in John 8:32 is more than merely being told. 'Then you will know the truth, and the truth will set you free.' The word 'know' is *gnōsesthe* (pronounced *NO-ses-the*) in koine Greek, one of the original languages of the New Testament (the second part of the Bible), and it means to perpetually learn and grasp more deeply and personally; to enquire and investigate in search of truth, especially spiritual truth.

The Beauty of Koine Greek

The New Testament was primarily written in ancient Greek (koine Greek) and has since been translated into approximately 2,255 languages. Koine Greek often has various, specific words where the English language has only one, all-encompassing word. The most famous example is koine Greek's many words for love, the most common being *agápe*, *éros*, *storge* and *philia*.

There are eleven koine Greek words for the verb 'to know'. *Gnōsesthe* is the one Jesus used when he said that we will know the truth and it will set us free.

For example, if you tell me your friend is kind, then in one sense I will know that your friend is kind. But if I get to know him personally, hear stories about his kindness and analyse his kindness in an attempt to better understand it – and if his kindness is driven by his spiritual relationship with God, and God is using it to reveal things to me over time, and I come to discover that his kindness is genuine enough for me to trust – that's when I will know that your friend is kind in the *gnōsesthe* way. *Gnōsesthe* is a journey of discovering and experiencing the truth, not a one-off, clinical exchange of information.

Think of some examples of things you have just been informed about versus things you know in a *gnōsesthe* way.

Info Knowledge	Gnõsesthe Knowledge

This course is designed to take you on a journey, through which you will discover and experience the truth of how addiction works in a *gnōsesthe* way, so that you can become free of it for good.

Addiction Is a Trick

Addiction is a con, a hustle, an illusion. One of the main reasons it is so successful is that we don't even realise we're being tricked . . . just like Tom. But once I found out that I was being tricked by my addiction and could see how the trick worked – when I finally knew the truth – the trick stopped working and I became free.

Since then I have shared that truth with many addicts, especially through the rehab programme my husband, Clyde, and I run in the UK, where we have witnessed many people becoming free. I have seen people who had previously gone round and round the abstinence–relapse cycle – dipping in and out of various rehab programmes – come to learn the truth and really know (*gnōsesthe*) it. They have subsequently told me, 'I haven't been tempted once since I got it' and 'I didn't know this kind of freedom was possible. I certainly didn't believe it was possible for me. But now I'm living it!' and 'I'm living proof that knowing the truth of how addiction works sets you free'. If you know how the trick works in a *gnōsesthe* way, you'll be unlikely to fall for it again.

What clever details did you notice about the way the con team tricked Tom?

....

....

....

Can you relate to any aspects of Tom's experience?

....

....

....

Even if you're not convinced by what I've written so far, keep going. Logic dictates that the only way to know whether we're being tricked or not is to have the trick explained. But for now, let's try a simple exercise. Use the next page to write down everything you value most in life. Go into detail. Rather than writing 'my kids', name each one. Rather than writing 'my sanity', note down everything that makes or keeps you sane. Once you've written everything you can think of, circle the five things you value most.

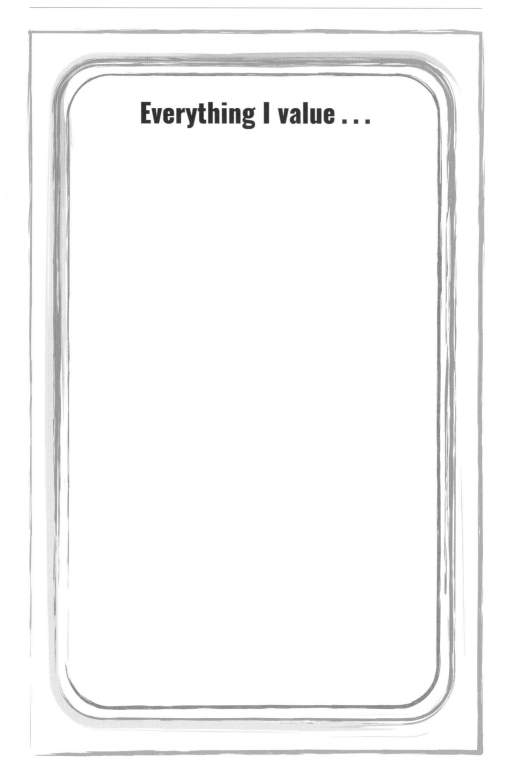

Everything I value . . .

Is the substance of your addiction among your top five values? Is it in your list at all? If not, are you prioritising something you don't even value? Is it possible that you are not only prioritising it over the things you value, but perhaps even forsaking or damaging the things you *do* value just to have the thing you *don't*?

Why do people jeopardise the things they truly love for something they don't even value? Are they being tricked? You may think, 'I do that because it's a disease.' We'll look into that later – scientifically, biblically and logically. Or you may say, 'I'm not really addicted. I can take it or leave it.' Well, I can take or leave broccoli, but if it caused any trouble for me or for others I'd leave it. For now, at least be willing to consider that you may have been tricked. If you desire, crave, need and use the activity or substance of your addiction because you're being tricked, it stands to reason that once you *gnōsesthe* you're being tricked and *gnōsesthe* how the trick works, you won't be tricked any longer. Therefore, you will no longer desire, crave, need or use that activity or substance again.

If the activity or substance of your addiction is among your list of what you value most (as I have known it to be for one person so far), you are as far into the trick as anyone can get. But there is still hope! And while you may feel as though it has some value to you, you wouldn't be holding this book in your hands if you didn't already know that your addiction isn't worth what it's costing you and others in various ways. If someone else put this book in your hands, you still value something more than the activity or substance if you are willing to read it – even if it is that very person.

'It made me feel alive, calm, loved, better. But now I need it to just feel close to normal.'

Addiction does exactly what those hustlers did. It distracts you with something seemingly positive while taking everything of value from you behind your back. It offers you a short, special moment, but then while your back is turned it takes away your whole future. But like Tom, the trick is so clever that you don't realise you're being robbed until it's too late. One moment you were getting high and felt distracted, but before you knew it you needed the drug just to make you feel less like you were dying. But you *are* dying, from self-poisoning. It's an evil trick; a poison in disguise.

> **A Trick Works Best When You Don't Realise It's Working**

The Ponzi scheme

When Phyllis and Jeremy heard that their neighbour, Darren, had accounting and investment experience, they paid him to invest some of their retirement money. When the initial results looked good they gave him more to invest, until all their savings were in his trusted hands, along with the savings of the friends and family members they had referred. Sadly, it turned out to be a Ponzi scheme, and they all lost everything.

Police and fraud experts advise that the best way to avoid investment fraud is to understand the tactics used. So it is with addiction.

Beware the psycho

What would you say to someone you care about who doesn't know how to end her relationship with a psycho who is destroying her life?

The psycho treated your loved one amazingly at first, showering her with gifts and attention, and saying everything perfectly in such a way that filled the gaps in her childhood.

The next thing you knew they were married. Gradually, over the next few years, the psycho started to ruin your loved one's career, alienated her from her friends and family, gaslighted and even assaulted her. The pyscho got stronger and stronger as he persistently did things to make her weaker and weaker.

Now the person you care about wants out, but she's terrified. She is also dependent on the psycho for everything, and she can't let go of the blissful experience they shared in the beginning.

Your drug is your psycho.

'But if it's a trick, maybe I want to stay tricked. Blissful ignorance, right?'

According to *The Perfectionism Book*, philosopher Robert Nozick asked a number of people if they would choose to be permanently hooked up to a machine that injected a feeling of great experiences – such as falling in love, achieving things, a child's laughter – but stopped them ever actually experiencing those things. The vast majority said no.[17]

But what if you went for it and the injection subtly changed from pleasurable to miserable experiences without you realising? What if the machine was gradually tricking your brain into thinking that pain was pleasure? Addictive substances alter the way the brain receives pleasure until you don't know what true pleasure is any more.

Uh oh!

Oh, wow!
That smells incredible.
I hope it's edible.
I want it *now*!

There it is. Yes!
Oh my, this sweet nectar is good.
I can't stop drinking, who would?
And it's even sweeter as it gets deeper.

I can barely think straight for how good this is.

Oh! My feet are slipping,
but no one could dismiss more of this.

Oh, no! I'm really slipping, and I don't know why.
When did it get so dark? Where's the sky?
Never mind, just a few more sips to try.
If I get too deep I'll just use my wings to fly,
It's not as though I'm actually going to . . .

What's that?
Is it . . . ?
It can't be.
It is!
It's others like me, except they're floating.

But I'll be okay.
I'm not gloating, but my wings are strong.
I don't belong with them, that's just wrong.
Besides, I won't stay too long.

Just a bit more.
Just . . . a little . . . bit . . . deeper,
Just a tiny bit more.
Just . . .

(Said the Fly of the Pitcher Plant)

What did it mean to you when you read that addiction may be a trick / con / illusion / hustle?

....

....

....

What choices can you make now to help you gain *gnōsesthe* knowledge?

....

....

....

Think of a time when someone harmed you by tricking you. What did they do?

....

....

....

If you found out you had been paying someone to steal from you, how would you react?

....

....

....

Think of all the ways that your addiction has been like a psychopath who romanced and seduced you, only to later isolate and destroy you. Be specific. How did it seduce you?

....

....

....

Of all that you value, what has your addiction taken or broken?

....

....

....

Phyllis and Jeremy's neighbour Darren stole the money they thought he was increasing. What did you think your addiction was increasing that you now see it has stolen?

....

....

....

In what ways can you relate to the fly in the poem?

....

....

....

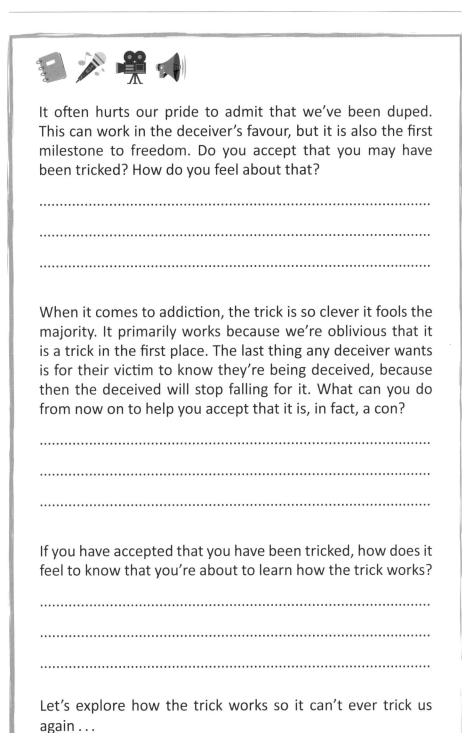

It often hurts our pride to admit that we've been duped. This can work in the deceiver's favour, but it is also the first milestone to freedom. Do you accept that you may have been tricked? How do you feel about that?

....

....

....

When it comes to addiction, the trick is so clever it fools the majority. It primarily works because we're oblivious that it is a trick in the first place. The last thing any deceiver wants is for their victim to know they're being deceived, because then the deceived will stop falling for it. What can you do from now on to help you accept that it is, in fact, a con?

....

....

....

If you have accepted that you have been tricked, how does it feel to know that you're about to learn how the trick works?

....

....

....

Let's explore how the trick works so it can't ever trick us again . . .

Dear God . . .

(For those who are not Christians)

. . . I'm very new to all this, but I'm willing to try it.

If you are real, I pray that you'll use this course to not only set me free from addiction, but to lead me to you.

Please help me to see you.

(For Christians)

. . . You are God, I am not. What a relief!

You know and see what I don't.

You even know me better than I know myself.

(For anyone)

. . . Thank you for this course. Thank you for everything I'm about to find out.

Thank you that I'm alive right now to do this; that it's not too late for me.

I confess that I'm really struggling. There are so many emotions right now, yet I feel numb at the same time.

I'm finding it pretty impossible to picture myself being free of this, but I'll let others – including the author of this course – believe it enough for both of us until I can believe it for myself.

Please help me complete this course and take in every milestone. Please help me know the truth that will set me free, and especially to know you – the ultimate truth.

Amen

You've achieved Milestone One!

Statement of truth:

I realise and accept that my choices, behaviour and feelings have been influenced by a con, and that I can break free from it by knowing and understanding how the con works.

'Then you will know the truth, and the truth will set you free'

John 8:32

Milestone Two:

Recognising That You Have
Been Hijacked, and How to
Find Your Way Back

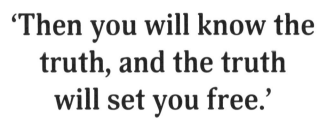

'Then you will know the
truth, and the truth
will set you free.'

John 8:32

Hijacked

This cruise had got off to an amazing start, even with just the bronze-level ticket. Sure, Theo and Davina couldn't enjoy the same quality of food and entertainment the gold-ticketholders had, but they didn't really know what they were missing out on, so it was all good.

Then one day, out of nowhere, they were suddenly blessed with all the trimmings. And not just gold quality, but full-on quantity as well. Theo and Davina lapped up the constant flow of food, entertainment and activities. They didn't even question it. Why would they draw attention to the fact that they were getting far more than they paid for? Everyone was having such fun, so they decided to just sit back and enjoy it.

By the early evening Davina realised she hadn't been up on deck all day. She hadn't even felt the sun on her skin. She figured it was probably empty up there since there was so much going on below deck. She didn't know how long she'd danced for, but the party was immense. It was so packed, she reckoned almost every single passenger must have been at that party. At the end of the night Davina fell into bed, exhausted!

The next morning she had planned to go up on deck for some sunshine, but someone was walking the corridors, shouting about what would be happening down in the entertainment room. She didn't want to miss that!

By lunchtime Davina had started to pick up on a few rumours that something was wrong. Apparently, a few people who had gone up on deck hadn't been seen since. Someone had heard that the ship had gone off course. She didn't pay much attention, though. What was the point in worrying? Some people always needed something to be negative about. She wanted to make the most of this incredible opportunity.

How was Davina to know that the ship had been hijacked? Those who had survived were now hostages, with no way of getting home. Sure, in retrospect she could see that all the food and fun had been used to manipulate and distract the passengers, but she wasn't the only one who hadn't seen it at the time. None of them had until it was too late.

Have you ever felt like that? As though one minute you were making the most of a fun situation, but before you knew it you were trapped?

By the time the passengers realised the ship was going in the wrong direction and they were in danger, they had begun to see the hijackers as their only hope of not drowning because the criminals had convinced them the ship would sink without them at the helm. Every so often a passenger considered resisting, maybe even fighting with the hijackers, but their fellow passengers soon reminded them that there was no point in trying. They did their best to console themselves with the new meagre rations and awkward, forced entertainment.

If a group of criminals wanted to hijack a cruise ship, their best method would involve mass manipulation and distraction. The ship is designed to please and entertain, so the hijackers would simply use that design to achieve their evil agenda. The criminals would first need to take out the legitimate captain and force the crew to follow new orders, but they would then use the ship's good team and good navigational design to fulfil their wicked purpose.

Addiction is the hijacker in this situation. It distracts our conscious from reasoning and evaluating, the way that the hijackers distracted the cruise passengers. While we are blissfully unaware, it overtakes the mechanisms of the brain and uses them to fulfil its bad purposes. It's like a hijacker using a ship's navigational design to go in the wrong direction. Essentially, addiction takes over the part of the brain that controls our impulses, the way that hijackers might take over the bridge control centre of a ship.

Are you beginning to recognise how the initial effects of your addiction distracted you from something bad taking control? How does that make you feel?

....

....

....

How often have you told yourself everything was fine, even though you knew deep down you were losing control?

....

....

....

Have you ever had 'fellow passengers' convince you there's no point resisting or fighting? Have you ever tried to convince others of that yourself? Why do you suppose people do that?

....

....

....

....

....

Can you relate the concept of the cruise ship passengers deciding that compliance with the hijacker is the lesser of two evils, given that the alternative is drowning in the ocean? Have you ever felt like you've lost control but decided that staying under the control of addiction is better than the alternative? What was that like?

....

....

....

....

....

What Does a Hijacking Look Like From the Control Centre?

The bridge of the cruise ship is like the subconscious mind. While the passengers have no awareness of what takes place in the bridge, it is the activity there that assesses, navigates and determines their destination, speed and more. If something went wrong in the control centre, the only way passengers could do anything about it would be to make themselves aware of what normally goes on in there.

In reality, understanding the conscious, unconscious and subconscious mind is much more complicated than this – too complicated even for qualified experts to be confident that they have a full understanding (there's even debate over differences between the unconscious and the subconscious, but I will mostly refer to the subconscious). But the basic concepts are demonstrated and declared in the Bible, and have also been examined and explained by science. For example, the conscious mind can alter the unconscious mind, but only once it becomes aware of what is happening there. Until we are consciously aware of what has formed at a subconscious level in our brains, we will continue to do what we hate doing and fail to do what we want to do.[1]

Until we know what is happening on the bridge of the cruise ship, we get distracted and end up being hijacked, heading in a direction we never intended to go. It is important to become aware of the subconscious in partnership with God, because there are various dangerous practices that can affect the subconscious mind in inappropriate ways, such as hypnosis, pagan rituals and extrasensory perception (ESP). The truth is, simple prayer, Bible reading and worship are the most healthy and productive ways for your conscious to become aware of what it needs to know. Safe counselling and learning from positive influences around us can also help.

The human brain is incredibly complex. In fact, it's a masterpiece of functional art. Even the most invested experts are still constantly discovering new things about it, and many of the more recent discoveries have called long-held beliefs about addiction into question.

It would not be helpful to go into the details of neuroscience (brain science) in these workbooks. For one thing, I am not a qualified neuroscientist or medic, and much more knowledgeable people have written on this subject. Furthermore, my goal is not to produce an academic paper on the science of addiction. Rather, it is to share truth that can set you free. But rest assured that I have read and listened to various experts, and the True Freedom website will recommend further reading for those who would like to understand the brain in greater detail, or for those seeking hard-and-fast evidence behind the truths I'm sharing with you. Recommended resources will also help those of you who are seeking a theological explanation in greater depth.

Without clear understanding and fully formed reasoning, our childhood experiences make imprints on our brains that can dictate our future without us realising it, and such things can have very negative effects. But when we let God reveal truth and highlight things to us we can partner with him and move towards freedom.

What stands out to you most from childhood that left an imprint on your brain which has negatively influenced the rest of your life? Once you've written your answers in this box, feel free to invite God to help you resolve these issues over time.

We will look at this in more detail later, but for now the important thing is to uncover enough truth to take back the power from your addiction. As we said earlier, if someone played a magic trick on you and took £10 from your account every time you fell for it, you'd soon want to know how the magician was doing it. And once you knew how the trick worked, you wouldn't fall for it any more. Well, this trick has taken more than little trickles of money from you, and it will keep taking until it has stolen everything. So, let's learn how the trick works so we can stop falling for it.

Happy Chemicals

Now we have a basic understanding that the subconscious mind is the control room and that it can be affected by the conscious mind, so long as the conscious mind is aware of it, we'll move on to dopamine. Don't worry if you're a bit confused – just get the gist for now and the pieces will soon fall into place. Sometimes the people who take longer to understand this trick end up with a stronger grip on the truth because they took more time to reread and process it. This truth is valuable enough for us to take our time over.

In simple terms, dopamine is one of the four main neurotransmitters, or 'happy chemicals', found in the brain. Dopamine makes you feel good, but addiction manipulates it. Addictive substances and activities also manipulate serotonin levels, so you feel increasingly depressed and anxious without them; oxytocin levels, so you fall in love with them to a certain degree; and endorphin levels to help manage pain and stress (though there is much debate over this one). It all matters but understanding how addiction affects dopamine levels in particular will help to reveal the trick we have discussed and set you free from your addiction.

Not only does a release of dopamine feel good, but it actually creates synapses – neural (brain) pathways that lead to us forming expectations, perspectives and beliefs, therefore affecting our subsequent behaviour. The reward centre of the brain uses dopamine to remember and communicate positive cause and effect.

God designed us this way so we're able to remember and return to good things, such as positive human affection, good food, laughter, the smell of flowers, and a mixture of hot sun and cool breeze on our skin. Things like a calm ocean view and the thrill of riding waves in a dancing sea. Like fresh drinking water when you're thirsty or a hot bath on a cold winter's day. Things like exhilarating times of worship, when you have to close windows and clear space because it's about to get loud and active, or when you see something in the Bible that you never saw before, or you hear the Holy Spirit speak to you in such a way that everything is forever altered for the better.

God wired our brains to remember and register that these things make us feel good so we'll be motivated to pursue them. This is especially powerful when we think of things that are good for us and make us feel great but that also take some effort, such as seeking and finding God at new levels, developing a healthy relationship, achieving something or making love.

Addiction hijacks this reward system and corrupts it. It creates a cycle of need and relief in the brain. Without the substance or activity of addiction there is no need for relief. It's a trick. But the real cruelty in terms of the damage addiction does to the brain – and the reason why its hijack tactic is so successful – is that it gradually reduces the amount of dopamine the brain releases from anything other than the substance or activity to which it is addicted. In time, the reward system no longer releases dopamine in response to laughter, friendship, fun, love and so on. This is why addicted parents can't bond with or enjoy their newborns; why addicts lose their libido outside of drug use or without sex itself being the drug; and why all previous hobbies and interests become boring and tedious.

On top of all that, the reward centre gradually ceases to release much dopamine from the substance or activity of your addiction, until one day all you can hope for is a meagre trickle from using that can't even compare with what non-addicts get from simply waking up. The overall dopamine deficit is at such a point of despair that this tiny lift of a hit feels like more than it really is (we'll discuss this in more detail in the next milestone).

Have you ever watched non-addicts and wondered why they're so happy without drugs? It's because their reward system isn't damaged.

Scientists have discovered that dopamine is triggered more by the anticipation of something rewarding than by the reward itself. Which makes sense, because it's all part of the reward system, and the brain is using it to learn what to pursue to gain pleasure. Something that feels good releases dopamine. The brain learns that this is something it wants to have more of and releases dopamine in anticipation.

Have you ever noticed how your withdrawal symptoms ease the moment you're holding a bag or a bottle? You haven't even taken anything yet, but simply knowing you're about to brings relief. Even just knowing your dealer is coming to meet you – or deciding to go and buy a bottle or gas can, to place a bet, to hook up or score – has the same effect. This is why intravenous addicts develop needle fixation. They are reacting to the dopamine released by the mere anticipation of the drug entering the body. But how can a thought or anticipation relieve physical symptoms? Because the physical symptoms are caused by what's happening in the brain, and because the drug / sex / bet / sugar isn't actually medicating you itself. Instead, your brain is doing what the drug (and you) have trained it to do. Your brain makes you ill when you've trained it to make you ill, and makes you feel better when you've trained it to feel better.

But then your dopamine (and serotonin) levels fall to a lower level than before you had the hit, leaving you worse off. The brain's reward system isn't designed to take notice of what brings you down. That's not its job. Its job is to register what makes you feel good. While the reward system is registering that the substance or activity triggers a release of dopamine (a good thing), your conscious mind – which should be detecting the fact that it also brings you lower after you have used it – is distracted and then in denial. Eventually, the brain is fully hijacked because the reward system is no longer triggered by anything else, and tons of faulty neural pathways have been formed to alter perspective and reactions, according to the brain's perceived desire for the substance or the addictive activity.

God designed this reward centre to bless us.

Addiction uses it against us.

Check out these pictures taken with imaging tools used by scientists and doctors: [2]

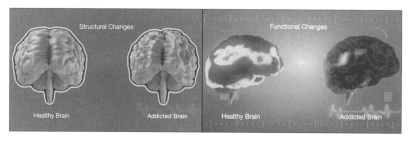

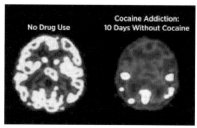

The damage is evident in these images. The trick is so cruel because it makes you think you're getting something, when the whole time it's actually taking the pleasure out of you. But . . . spoiler alert! Science also proves what God has long let us in on. The brain can heal! Scientists call it neuroplasticity, while the Bible calls it transformation through renewal. We'll get into all that a bit later.

Had you given much thought to the workings of your subconscious mind before? What difference do you think this awareness will make from now on?

....

....

....

Give some examples of positive things your conscious thoughts are feeding into your subconscious (maybe thoughts regarding loved ones, God, future dreams, etc.).

....

....

....

....

Now give some examples of negative thoughts feeding into your subconscious.

....

....

....

....

In what ways does your experience of the substance or compulsive behaviour of your addiction line up with the science of dopamine and the reward system? Do you have any specific memories that relate to what you've just learned?

....

....

....

....

....

What did you derive joy and pleasure from before addiction that you no longer derive joy or pleasure from?

....

....

....

....

Can you think of any other things God has designed for good that have been abused and used for bad?

....

....

....

....

What came to your mind when you first saw the brain images?

....

....

....

How did you feel when you read that the brain can heal?

....

....

....

What Exactly Are Neural Pathways?

Neuroscientist Dr Caroline Leaf says they look like interconnected tree branches. In her book, *Who Switched Off my Brain?*, she explains in scientific terms that the tree is either healthy or toxic.[3] Neural pathways are the connections our brains make based on our behaviour, which then go on to influence our behaviour. In their book, *Keys to Health, Wholeness & Fruitfulness*, Dr Goss and Dr Wren use the example of a Land Rover travelling on muddy ground to illustrate how brain pathways work.[4] If the vehicle repeats a journey over and over until the tire tracks become hardened by the sunshine, the car will eventually follow the ingrained route, even if the driver lets go of the steering wheel.

Another way to comprehend neural pathways is to think of a watercourse on a mountain. The more times the rain follows that course, the deeper the groove in the land gets. The deeper the groove gets, the more the water is directed that way, until it becomes much more than a groove and successfully provokes rainwater to run that way. Eventually, the majority of rainwater that falls onto the mountain ends up taking that course because the passage has formed so deeply.

The average brain processes 400 billion actions per second. That's like 400 billion raindrops looking for a direction to travel down the mountain. When someone's reward centre is hijacked by an addictive substance, the dopamine sends messages to create pathways (like a watercourse down a mountain) that increasingly send them to one conclusion: I need to use. So, a rainfall of *good* news is guided by a desire to celebrate by 'treating yourself' to poison. A rainfall of *bad* news is directed to a desire to console yourself with that poison. The rainfall of boredom, fun, stress, excitement, friends, enemies, this place, that activity, and eventually every place and every activity are all directed to the same location, despite it being a target for utterly opposing results.

Whether you need celebration, comfort, stimulation, relaxation, distraction or focus, the hijacked brain erroneously creates a pathway which subsequently tells you that one deceptive thing can meet all those needs. The deepening pathways cause more and more activity to go one way, pointing you to the substance or activity of your addiction.

Neural (brain) pathways

Our thoughts are not invisible, ethereal or airy-fairy nonentities; they are physical activities in the brain, they are physical pathways we can look at in scans. Brain scans reveal that pathways can look drastically different, depending on whether they are healthy or unhealthy.

God already knew all this when he inspired Solomon, the wisest man on earth, to say that we become what we think in our hearts.[5] It's no wonder the Bible exhorts us think about whatever is true, noble, right, pure, lovely, admirable, excellent and praiseworthy.[6]

These subconscious pathways your addiction builds – which then go on to further build your addiction – are a big part of what we need to understand in order to reverse the damage and recover.

When I first started learning to drive, it was an entirely conscious process. It took a lot of thought, and I couldn't imagine ever doing it without concentrating. But once I had developed the neural pathways for driving, the mechanical side of it became largely subconscious, so that my conscious could be thinking about anything and pay no attention at all to my pedals or gears because my subconscious was doing it without my conscious being involved. I could subconsciously signal, accelerate, brake and perceive hazards while consciously belting out my favourite song on stage in front of Simon Cowell, who wanted to know more about the Christian lyrics that had struck him so powerfully. The imagination is a powerful part of our conscious, and it takes great depths of imagination to conceive that I'd ever find myself singing on a stage!

But if I went to another country and needed to drive on the opposite side of the road, I would have to draw my driving practices out of my subconscious and into my conscious, where I can alter them accordingly. No television singing now; in fact, no singing at all while I'm concentrating so hard on the driving. It would take conscious effort and be quite difficult to go against my subconscious programming. But if I stayed in the other country, driving on that side of the road would become subconsciously ingrained before long, and I would soon be doing it without engaging my conscious mind. Back to the stage I go! So it is with walking, eating and more complex things – everything else, good or bad, that we learn until it becomes second nature.

Addiction works the same way. Following a pathway to whatever has addicted you is ingrained subconscious programming that controls you without you even thinking about it. In order to alter that programming, you need to bring it back into your conscious mind. The good news is, you're doing that right now simply by engaging with these workbooks. It will take time and conscious effort to change the pathways, but before long the new way will become subconsciously ingrained and you'll be doing that without thinking. If you follow the correct process, you will suddenly realise one day that you haven't had a craving in a while. Then you will realise that you went somewhere, saw someone or went through something that would have prompted you to use before, but this time you didn't even think about it.

However, addiction is not merely a habit. If it were just a habit, it would be as easy to change as it is to drive on the other side of the road in another country. The idea of addiction as a habit is what inspires the scary images on cigarette packets, as if the threat of death could force habit change. Only it doesn't work, because addiction is not just a habit. There is certainly an overlap between habit and addiction, because both involve neural pathways, but they are not the same because habits don't hijack the reward system of the brain the way addiction does.

Did you know that the way you think physically alters your brain and therefore directs your choices, attitudes and behaviour? How does that impact the way you think about your thoughts?

....

....

....

....

Did you have any idea that your thoughts and the dopamine in your brain create pathways that direct your responses in certain directions? How does this make you feel about all the times you've felt driven to use, even when your conscious mind had previously decided not to?

....

....

....

....

What positive activities or reactions can you think of that you now realise are driven by subconscious pathways?

....

....

....

What Is Cognitive Dissonance?

So far we have looked at dopamine and neural pathways. Cognitive dissonance is the third and final key to understanding how addiction takes over. Cognitive dissonance refers to the anguish created when a person engages in behaviours or activities that are in conflict with their beliefs and perspectives. This puts the brain in conflict with itself, which impacts negatively on their mental and emotional wellbeing. When the brain is in conflict, it takes the path of least resistance. It will choose what we have most persistently trained it to choose.

Jesus was referring to money when he said that no man can serve two masters because he'll ultimately love one and hate the other.[7] But I wonder if he also had in mind these workings of the brain he had created. The brain cannot perpetually be at war with itself. It cannot serve two masters. It cannot love an action and love a person that the action harms. It cannot hold to a moral belief while indefinitely behaving in a way that is contrary to it, or receive full pleasure from something that works against the person's conscience. The brain may even shut down parts of itself in order to reduce conflict.

I remember a study I read, which gives a really helpful example of this. The study showed that when a man masturbates while watching porn, he cannot have a guilty conscience about the likelihood of sex-trafficking or abuse while enjoying satisfactory pleasure, so the brain has to choose – conscience or pleasure. By the very physical act of continuing to masturbate, the man (the same would apply to women, but the study only included men) is telling his brain that pleasure takes precedence over the conscience, so the brain follows the command. Brain scans have indicated that the part of the brain that produces empathy literally shuts down while people are masturbating to porn.[8] You can imagine the impact this has on the brain over time. I am not aware of the same tests being done on brains during the physical act of using a substance or engaging in an addictive activity, but given the way cognitive dissonance works, it stands to reason that the same thing would happen.

How does this apply to you? Well, for one thing it explains why you've done things you never thought your conscience would allow you to do. It explains how you have been able to choose your addiction over the people it is hurting. You are not some kind of evil freak; you have simply done things the addiction hijacked your brain's design to do. There was a powerlessness to it. But now that you are learning how your addiction has tricked you, you can start to regain control over your brain and your whole body.

Do you remember the first time you felt the anguish of cognitive dissonance, when the substance or activity you were about to engage in went against what you believed or loved? What was that like? What happened?

....

....

....

Can you describe the last time you felt the anguish of cognitive dissonance – whether you were submitting to the addiction or resisting it?

....

....

....

The Road to Recovery

During the recovery process, we force our brains to become conflicted. We prevent them from taking the path of least resistance and force them not to follow the path we formerly trained them to follow. Short of a miracle (we'll discuss those later), there is no way that it won't be awkward, uncomfortable and even painful for a while. There will likely be deep angst.

Your whole body may feel awkward. You may feel disconnected from anything and everything. You may feel lost, empty and almost soulless, yet painfully deep at the same time; awkwardly distant and yet horribly close. Exposed, weak, angry, sad and confused. It may feel like a hundred people are screaming at once in your mind, yet somehow your thoughts are inaudible. All the while, sleep either proves impossible or you are riddled with nightmares. Or perhaps sleep is the only thing you are able to do.

But remember that this is a phase, a short chapter in your life. It is an essential bit of terrain on the journey to freedom, like the pain of yanking a compound-fractured bone in order to set it back in place.

I said a moment ago that the brain will always choose what we have most persistently trained it to choose. The ongoing act of surrender to addiction trains the brain to choose that thing over anything and anyone else. But that also means we can train the brain to persistently choose well. Not only can we train the brain to choose the right things over the trick our addiction has played on us, but over time – as we recover and learn and grow – we will be able to train our brains to persistently choose well in all areas of life.

Why Doesn't Everyone Get Addicted?

Having learned the ways that addiction corrupts the brain by hijacking the reward system and using it to create pathways that drive you back to it time and time again, with less and less resistance, you may be wondering how it is that some people use a drug and don't end up in a downward spiral of addiction. Perhaps you have heard about men who were given heroin during the Vietnam War, for example.[9]

Many variables reduce the likelihood of someone becoming addicted to a substance, but the main factor is having a range of activities in our lives that create healthy dopamine release. Coupled with strong beliefs about self and others, which repel repetitive use at a neurological level, these factors work together to leave a person with little to escape from or to make the substance's dopamine rush less impactful. Additionally, people who take drugs 'experimentally' are less likely to spiral into the depths of addiction if their brains haven't already been exposed to addictive substances such as nicotine, alcohol, refined sugars and cannabis, or repetitive addicting activities such as masturbation or gaming.

For the soldiers who were given heroin, the effect was more overt, from the instant quick capture to the dramatic drop. It was a distraction of mass intensity and a fast-spiralling con of dramatic proportions. The soldiers were studied for ongoing responses after returning home, and those who didn't continue to use were almost always the ones who had a huge dopamine rush simply from returning home. That, coupled with the drastic reaction heroin creates, meant it was harder for the addiction to distract and trick their conscious minds from what was happening and easier for their brains to primarily associate drug use with the horrors of war. Additionally, people were less exposed to more subtle invasions of hijacking addiction at a young age back then, such as from highly processed foods, porn, smartphones and gaming.

Addictions such as nicotine and sugar involve a more subtle enticement over time, often using bait so subtle that the conscious mind doesn't register it, as it is distracted by the coughing from the smoke (which it doesn't register as a negative) or the taste of the treat. But the brain records what has just happened, and when the dopamine drop comes, the brain will assume the same thing that lifted it an hour ago will lift it again. So the pathways begin to gain traction while the conscious mind is unaware of what is happening.

Almost every addict started off being subtly tricked. People do not generally wake up one day having never smoked, drunk alcohol or taken addictive prescription meds, and say to themselves, 'I'm going to try heroin today!' The brain can't be tricked that easily by something so obvious. No, most people begin using 'gateway drugs' or socially acceptable activities, convinced they'd never do something like that each time they do the last thing they said they'd never do. In cases where children are given intense-reaction substances, their brains aren't even formed yet and their living contexts are unlikely to be producing healthy dopamine release. It is the subtlety of the indirect substances – often combined with difficult circumstances – that allow the brain to be subtly hijacked and trigger the damage under the radar.

If these subtle dopamine fixes have already started training the brain towards addiction, the hijacking process has begun – the passengers just don't know it yet. Some may never step beyond this subtle hijacking. They may live in a context in which they are never exposed to hard drugs or high-cost activities such as gambling. Or they may live in an environment so full of healthy dopamine triggers, such as love, achievement and community, that the reward centre is substantially satisfied. People like this may catch the hijacker early and regain control of the ship, while others simply sink down the pitcher plant more gradually through the slow burn of less aggressive substances and activities. In any and all cases, addiction is the same. All humans are susceptible to it, because it works and succeeds by hijacking the reward system and using the gift we have all been given against us.

Here Comes the Really Good News!

There's a process that scientists call 'neuroplasticity'. The Bible calls it 'transformation'. Romans 12:2 tells us not to conform to the patterns of this world, but to be transformed by the renewing of our minds. You have already started doing that, simply by engaging in this course. And you will do it even more successfully when you start taking your thoughts captive in obedience to Christ. We will look at the practicalities of this in Part Two, which will take your recovery to a whole new level. But for now, check out the evidence of the transformation or neuroplasticity in the pictures below.[10] This is possible for you!

Here we see that the brain is literally being restored during the recovery process.

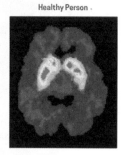
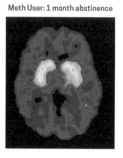
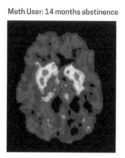

The difference between 10 and 100 days proves that the brain can heal back.

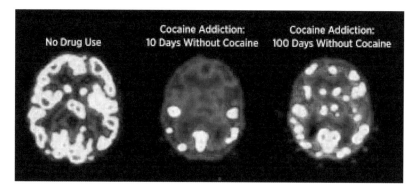

At the beginning of this milestone, I said that addiction takes out the current captain of our lives, which is usually ourselves. But this course doesn't just give you the opportunity to remove the hijacker once and for all; it also gives you the opportunity to make Jesus your new captain. There's no better captain of our lives than Jesus, because he is all-knowing, all-powerful and all-loving, which we are not.

This means that if we make him captain we can far exceed the mere existence of being 'clean and dry', and instead enjoy a full life, which we'll delve into in Part Two.

Let me offer you one amazing thought to take away from this milestone. By learning what you need to do to reverse the brain damage of addiction, you're equipping yourself with truth that can work in your favour for the rest of your life; a truth that non-addicts also need but won't necessarily learn in the powerful way you will. Addiction doesn't have to be the end of your story. God can turn your life around and could even help you use your experience of addiction for good.

'And we know that in all things God works for the good of those who love him, who have been called according to his purpose' (Romans 8:28).

Dear God . . .

(For those who are not Christians)

. . . Once again, if you are real, please use this course to not only set me free from addiction, but to lead me to you.

Please help me to see you.

(For anyone)

. . . You are God, I am not. What a relief!

You know every hair on my head, every pathway in my brain, every fibre of my being.

Thank you for intricately designing my brain for my good.

Thank you for graciously giving me the gift of neuroplasticity, allowing me to partner with you to fix my own damage.

I confess that I am so far from invincible and in control that the gift you gave me has been used against me, and therefore also against you.

I ask that you would help me to use your gift well, to take responsibility for my own conscious thoughts and to use them to immerse myself in truth. I also pray for supernatural help on this journey.

Amen

You've achieved Milestone Two!

Statement of truth:

I realise that addiction is a type of brain damage, but that God gave my brain the ability to heal when his amazing design is hijacked.

'Then you will know the truth, and the truth will set you free'

John 8:32

Milestone Three:

Discovering What Causes Cravings
and How to Make Them Stop

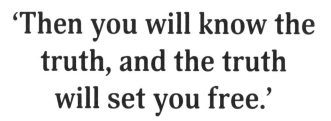

'Then you will know the
truth, and the truth
will set you free.'

John 8:32

Cravings

What is a craving? Well, on a conscious level, it's an 'I *have* to have it now!' feeling, which comes with a whole load of physical and psychological angst or torment, especially if the craving isn't relieved quickly. It's even worse if you're trying to fight the craving without understanding what it is on a subconscious level. So, let's deal with that. Let's bring this issue clearly into our conscious brains.

Time and time again, I have seen people amazed by how much their cravings have changed once they understood them better. I couldn't believe how easy it became for me to deal with the cravings that had previously made me feel utterly powerless and hopeless once I knew the truth.

On the next page you will see a graph I created to explain how the brain's reward system relates to the way you feel. People living with addiction who saw this graph before the book was published were struck by how strongly they related to it, and my memory of addiction also relates to it. The reality is so vivid that both Allen Carr and Neil T. Anderson have described or created their own versions in their own books about addiction.[11] Seeing it drawn out can be so liberating, as it brings clarity to the experience.

Craving is the feeling created by an addicted brain, and here is how it works:

START HERE

Ultimate Euphoria

Dopamine and serotonin levels fall to a lower level than before you used.

Whether it's registering a drastic high from narcotics or a subtler one from nicotine, the brain has grasped the cause and effect of using the substance in question.

The real cruelty of it all is that we're designed to enjoy these highs, but through relationship with God, which we are rarely exposed to from a young age. Often a counterfeit for God offers to take us there instead.

The highs never get as high as they did at first. But the reward system has done its job in registering cause and effect. Its design has been hijacked.

Baseline

The first hit

The reward system doesn't realise that the substance is bringing you down each time you use and making you feel lower overall. It just knows that whatever it is gives you an instant lift, so it acts on that.

At this point, your brain says, 'I know what made me feel better earlier.' Then it asks for more of that.

Different substances and activities may vary in terms of the high and low, but the brain reacts in the same way, and the overall pattern is very similar.

Repetition trains your brain to see another fix as a solution for your next low.

We're not just chasing the first high; we're chasing the last one, because the next one is always less impactful . . .

The lower you feel, the more your hijacked reward system seeks the thing it believes to be lifting you up.

. . . until every 'high' is nothing more than a small improvement on the lowest low.

At this point you start to notice that the upward lines are getting shorter and the downward lines are getting longer. But in reality, I started shortening the up lines and lengthening the down lines early on, so subtly that you didn't notice. Addiction does exactly the same thing. At first you don't realise the decline . . . and by the time you do, it's too late.

'I only use to feel normal,' you say. But this type of despair is *not* normal.

Utter Despair

Munchausen Syndrome by Proxy

Have you ever heard of Munchausen syndrome by proxy? These days it is officially called factitious disorder imposed on another (FDIA), but it's a psychological condition where a person either pretends that someone in their care is sick or actively makes them sick. Even though this is a form of mental illness, serious criminal charges can be brought against anyone convicted of such abuse. Can you imagine being so ill that you need constant help to survive, and then finding out that the person you thought was helping you was actually the one making you so ill in the first place?

The truth is, you don't need to imagine it. Your addiction has been giving you the impression that it is helping you cope, when in actual fact it is the cause of your need for help. Using a substance or activity of addiction appears to cure the very illness it is creating. But every snort, dig, bet, smoke, jab, swallow, binge and dysfunctional orgasm that spikes a high on the graph drags you lower than you felt before you experienced it. Every hit creates a need for the next hit.

Most of us enter addiction with suffering already present inside us. As a result, we mistakenly think that the drug helped soothe the problem or helped us escape from it. Think about it . . . people who don't take drugs or do other addictive things go through grief, overcome trauma and gradually get better. For addicts, the pain and sorrow only gets worse every time they are sober. That's because it doesn't actually help with the pain at all; it merely distracts them with a temporary euphoria while it creates a whole new problem that it tricked your brain into thinking only it could solve. That's what craving is.

Imagine that a Munchausen by proxy victim had already been legitimately sick before the guardian started making them sick in a new way. Pre-existing sickness makes the guardian's deception easier and more successful. So it is with our original sorrow and the sorrow the drugs and compulsive behaviours create in us.

Within the graph shown on the next page, write down any memories you have from your experience of different parts of the downward slide. Record your memories of high and low points.

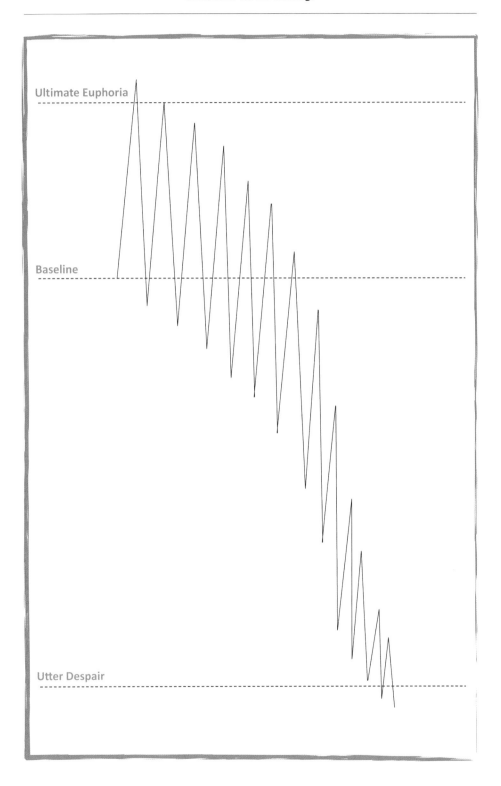

Do the good memories outweigh the bad ones? What stands out most from these memories of highs and lows.

....

....

....

....

....

Have you been trying to chase that first high ever since you experienced it? Or have you reached the point of just using to feel less awful?

....

....

....

....

How would you react if you were seriously ill and you found out that the person you thought had been taking care of you was actually the one making you ill in the first place?

....

....

....

....

....

How do you feel about the substance or act of your addiction now that you realise it has actually been causing the problem you thought it was fixing?

....

....

....

....

....

The craving is at its worst and most tormenting when we're forcing it to undergo cognitive dissonance, when the conscious awareness of truth fights against the subconscious pathways forged over years of false impression. Even most non-addicts and pre-addicts are subject to misinformation about addiction and substances from news reports, comments in a favourite sitcom, storylines in a soap, conversations going on around us and more. At this stage it's like a fight is taking place in the mind – a mental tug of war – but it's actually a physiological battle taking place in our physical brains.

Taking thoughts captive, forging new pathways and pushing back an established lie with a new truth is not always easy or sudden. In fact, it's usually a painful process. We will see why that's not such a bad thing in Part Two, but for now we can simply say that it is necessary, temporary and productive. When armed with the transforming power of knowledge and truth, the process is not one of ongoing misery, but rather a patch of bad road along a generally good journey. It's like when someone has a dislocated shoulder popped back in. The pain of the joint relocation is more excruciating than the dislocation, but it's an essential and temporary pain to end the ongoing suffering.

Below is a graph that demonstrates how craving works during the early stages of withdrawal. It is not so much the drug or act you are withdrawing from, but the dopamine (and serotonin) fix that has, over time, become your brain's only form of dopamine release. Until your brain has a chance to start healing, there will most likely be a period of dopamine deficit, during which time your brain cannot release the primary chemicals that contribute to good mood. There are times when God circumvents this natural process and supernaturally creates relief – I have seen that many times – but he knows that the benefits of going through the natural process often outweigh the relief of avoiding it.

Just as the downward spiral was a process, so is getting back up. For most people, recovery happens in the reverse of deterioration; restoration happens in the reverse of loss; and freedom happens in the reverse of mental hijacking. This means that it starts at the very bottom, when we are at our weakest, with our own brains working against us. But this graph shows you that the miserable part won't last. This is the time to take each day at a time.

Read these text boxes from the bottom of the page up

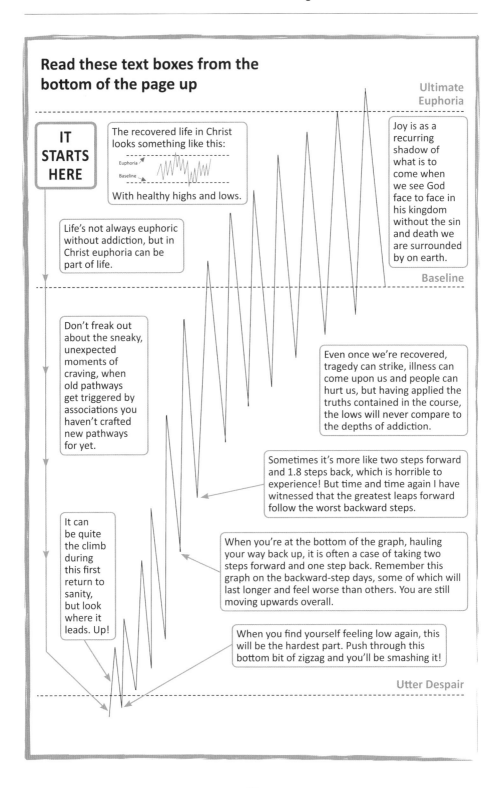

Ultimate Euphoria

IT STARTS HERE

The recovered life in Christ looks something like this:

Euphoria

Baseline

With healthy highs and lows.

Joy is as a recurring shadow of what is to come when we see God face to face in his kingdom without the sin and death we are surrounded by on earth.

Baseline

Life's not always euphoric without addiction, but in Christ euphoria can be part of life.

Don't freak out about the sneaky, unexpected moments of craving, when old pathways get triggered by associations you haven't crafted new pathways for yet.

Even once we're recovered, tragedy can strike, illness can come upon us and people can hurt us, but having applied the truths contained in the course, the lows will never compare to the depths of addiction.

Sometimes it's more like two steps forward and 1.8 steps back, which is horrible to experience! But time and time again I have witnessed that the greatest leaps forward follow the worst backward steps.

It can be quite the climb during this first return to sanity, but look where it leads. Up!

When you're at the bottom of the graph, hauling your way back up, it is often a case of taking two steps forward and one step back. Remember this graph on the backward-step days, some of which will last longer and feel worse than others. You are still moving upwards overall.

When you find yourself feeling low again, this will be the hardest part. Push through this bottom bit of zigzag and you'll be smashing it!

Utter Despair

Don't Believe the Lies

Recovery can be extremely difficult at first, because not only are you still feeling very low, but it is from that low place that you are fighting the programmed pathways in your brain. Your temporarily damaged brain is unable to produce the feel-good chemicals that non-addicts experience every day. Feel-good chemicals you can only get tiny amounts of from your addiction – for now! But once you know (*gnōsesthe*) that this is just the first part of a process that will lead to freedom, you will find a way to do it.

The addiction will fight you and the compulsion will feel so strong that your mind will tell you, 'This is too hard to keep doing day after day, week after week, month after month. You may as well give up now. It's better to give up now than suffer like this for months and then fall anyway, making it all a waste.' But once you know it won't last that long, and that such thoughts are created by the drug's hijack of your brain's reward system, the programming of pathways, and the trick being played on your mind, you can dispute them as the lies they are. You'll be able to see that you *will* ultimately get better and better, until soon you'll be over the worst of it. Providing you are partnering with God (which we will look at in Part Two) and in an environment that promotes inner healing, you will, in time, feel better than you ever have before. In the end, you will perpetually live at the top of the graph, where bad is OK and good is great.

This graph will act as the reminder you need to keep going. It's also worth remembering that you're only down at the bottom because of the drug that tricked you, and you're only experiencing cravings because that drug hijacked your brain. Merely by thinking about the truth, you are changing pathways so your brain can heal.

The Holiday Balcony

Remember what I said in the graph about not freaking out in response to sneaky, unexpected moments of craving further down the road to recovery? Well, I'll never forget the day my husband and I arrived at our holiday hotel one year, when my knowledge of the truth was truly put to the test.

We had landed, checked in at reception, walked around the resort to our block with our cases and stopped at the bottom of the staircase to our room.

'This is ours,' my husband and I said in unison, and chuckled.

It was beautifully hot and bright, with a lovely, gentle breeze. I could already feel the vitamin D being sucked in by my skin and hear the distant sounds of laughter from around the pool. As we started walking up the external spiral staircase, I looked up to what I assumed was our room. I saw the balcony and thought, 'That's where I can smoke.'

What?! Smoke?

I hadn't smoked for such a long time that I couldn't even remember the last time I had thought of it. Where had this thought come from? A genuine desire? Missing the cigarettes? Feeling like a holiday wouldn't be the same without smoking?

No! It had surfaced because the very act of being on holiday triggered an old neural pathway that I hadn't had a chance to replace. After all, it's not every day you go on holiday. I had created a pathway in my brain that associated balconies with smoking, especially since I had lived in an apartment with a balcony where I smoked during a very dark time in my life, which had left a deep impression. Each drag of nicotine and sip of alcohol felt like such a relief. Of course it wasn't real relief, it was an illusion, but that doesn't just make an old pathway disappear. My brain still had that association between balconies and smoking, but it only took me about one second to know that. I had one second of panic, then literally laughed out loud. I chuckled to myself with real joy that the old lie couldn't trick me any more.

Time and time again, I had been sideswiped by these unexpected cravings of one drug or another before I knew the truth, and I had falsely assumed that the craving was a genuine desire. Very often this led to relapse because I would start thinking about why I wanted the substance and feel discouraged that I still desired it, which would open up old, disused pathways and drag me back in. But this holiday memory is a prime example of a time when I found it so easy that I laughed because I knew the truth.

Craving is the feeling created by faulty brain activity when the truth hasn't been applied to any given trigger pathway. You will experience a craving in response to every trigger that hasn't yet received a new pathway. When this happens, remember that it's just an automatic brain reaction, not a heart's desire. In the early days of recovery, and especially through the withdrawal process, there are so many pathways triggering you to use that it can feel like a continuous and painful resistance, but that will soon ease. Some of the pathways will fizzle out really quickly. Others are more stubborn, while others are forgotten altogether until something prompts them, like the holiday balcony.

Ingraining the Truth

Craving doesn't have to take you anywhere near relapse. Relapse only happens when the truth hasn't been applied.

Cravings can come gradually – by resurrecting and strengthening old faulty pathways through thoughts and imaginings – or suddenly, when a trauma or shock temporarily makes the newer truth pathways harder to access. But the more ingrained the truth becomes the stronger it is in any circumstance. People who are fully recovered from addiction can face any trial or tragedy without even thinking about using. I have seen it more times than I can count. And I am living it myself.

For some people, the truth penetrates deeply straight away, or there's a supernatural impact and then freedom comes quickly. For others it can take up to five years, which isn't all that surprising when you consider all the damage, faulty perspectives and lifestyle patterns that came with and from the addiction, which also need to be overcome. In any case, there is no biblical, scientific or logical reason to desire a destructive substance or activity for the rest of your life.

There is a degree to which you may still crave a sense of escapism, but people who have never been addicted to anything can also crave that. It's part of our sinful human nature (which we'll discuss in Part Two). But former addicts who truly understand the trick and apply the teachings in this course will be less susceptible to the trick than someone who has never used a drug in their lives. It's like someone banging their head on a low door frame. That person is much less likely to do it again than someone who hasn't gone through the doorway yet. You can use the same reward–learn–act mechanism of the brain that addiction tricked you with to stop it ever tricking you again.

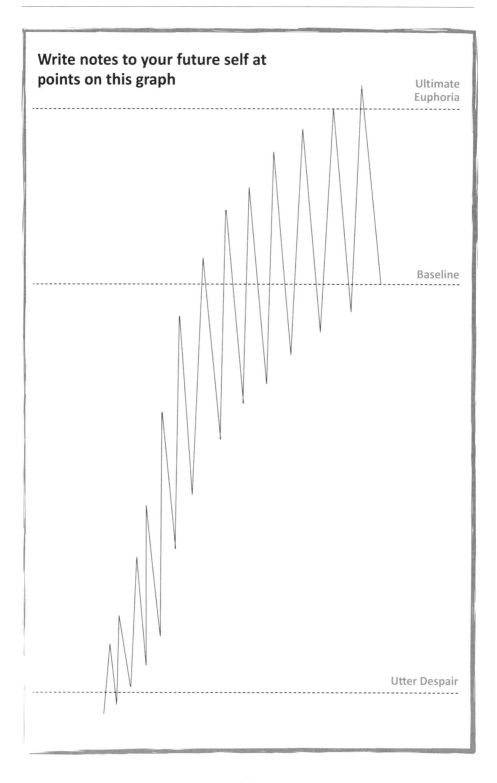

Which bits of this milestone stood out to you the most?

....

....

....

Which Bible verse – or memorable quote – will you memorise to help you remember what you need to do during the darkest moments of craving, and also during the sneaky, unexpected moments of craving?

....

....

....

Which paragraphs or sentences from this book so far will you memorise to help you remember what you need to do during the darkest moments of craving, and also during the sneaky, unexpected moments of craving?

....

....

....

Create Your Own Statement of Truth

Use the next page to create a poster of your own statement of truth – a statement that combines your answers above in one sentence to remind you of the truth. Cut out this page and put it somewhere visible – such as the bathroom mirror – so it really sinks in.

You can use the space on this page to draft and craft your impactful statement for the poster.

My Statement of Truth

Dear God . . .

(For those who are not Christians)

. . . I'm still not sure about you yet, but I'm going to keep going and see what happens.

Please help me to see you.

(For anyone)

. . . You are God, I am not.

Jesus, my worst cravings can't compare to how badly you must have wanted to escape as the torturous death ahead of you was so daunting that you literally sweated blood from the anxiety of it. Yet you didn't escape. You faced death head-on and won the victory so that I can also have the victory. You are amazing!

Thank you for the truth. Thank you for helping me see that craving is temporary if I face it head-on, and that the only way to end it is to end the cause of it. Thank you for leading me to discover that [insert the name of your addictive substance or behaviour] has been pretending to cure the illness it has been giving me all along.

I confess that I am weak and that I need your strength.

Please help me focus and give me the courage to persevere through this ugly part of a beautiful road. Please open my heart to receive supernatural joy in the valley of happiness deficit. Holy Spirit, if my own broken mind screams defeatist hopelessness at me, please remind me of the graphs, the picture of progress and phases, and my statement of truth.

Amen

You've achieved Milestone Three!

Statement of truth:

I recognise that a craving is the feeling caused by faulty brain activity, and a vicious cycle in which every use makes me need the next use. I understand that using continues the craving, while not using stops it.

'Then you will know the truth, and the truth will set you free'

John 8:32

Milestone Four:

Using Willpower in the
Short Term to Experience
Freedom in the Long Term

'Then you will know the truth, and the truth will set you free.'

John 8:32

Willpower

In Roald Dahl's classic children's story *The Witches*, the evil characters seeking children as their prey appear to be ordinary women. The children see beautiful, kind women offering them sweets and treats, but in reality the witches are ugly and frightening-looking, with clawed hands, horrible feet, bald heads and oversized nostrils. When the children see these witches in their true form, they are frightened by the evil and want to get as far away from them as possible. It's only when the witches appear in disguise that the children are lured in.

Likewise, the deception of addiction makes something hideously ugly appear beautiful to lure us in. It makes something murderous appear like rescue and something repulsive appear irresistible. We only need to rely on willpower to abstain from addictive activities or substances while we're still seeing the false beauty, rescue and irresistibility in something that is actually hideous, murderous and repulsive. Once the lens of distortion is removed, no willpower is needed to abstain because the desire for it is gone.

It breaks my heart to see social media statuses, watch TV characters and meet people who are painfully denying themselves something every day that they wouldn't even want if they knew it for what it really was. But unlike the children who are eventually able to see that the 'kind women' offering them treats are actually evil witches they should run away from, the deception of addiction runs considerably deeper. It is far crueller and much harder to watch.

To abstain from something is 'to not do something, especially something enjoyable that you think might be bad'[12] or to 'restrain oneself from doing or enjoying something'.[13] Therefore, abstinence is about denying yourself something you want; something enjoyable. This requires willpower – a 'strong determination that allows one to do something difficult'[14] – because you are constantly having to say no to something you want.

We have already learned that resisting the source of addiction is only difficult while under the illusion of the trick, and we now know that the activity or substance of the addiction is only desirable because we have been tricked in terms of its desirability. Therefore, willpower becomes increasingly redundant against addiction as the truth becomes known. I don't have to abstain from Turkish Delight because I can't stand the stuff. I have no desire for it. I think it's safe to assume that none of us have to abstain from eating vomit off the roadside, because doing so has no appeal. As the truth is known, the addictive substance or activity loses its appeal. It stops being something we need to resist and becomes an easy choice that requires no willpower at all.

The Elephant in the Camp

Once we have learned how the illusion works and got the upper hand over it, we realise it is not really enjoyable, beneficial or desirable, and we don't actually want it. It's heartbreaking when people remain tricked by addiction and have to abstain from the illusion-created desire, miserably and painstakingly, when they could be set free from it for good if they realised it was a trick. Sure, teeth-gritting resistance is a better option than the destructive effects of surrender to a substance or compulsive behaviour that would destroy multiple lives, but that's a low bar. And it's very sad when you know that the truth could solve the problem altogether by removing the fake appearance of anything good so that any desire left for it is completely removed.

There's a famous short story about a man who was walking past an elephant camp. He noticed the elephants weren't being kept in cages or kept on chains. All that was holding them back from escape was a small piece of rope tied to one leg. As the man gazed at the elephants, he was completely confused as to why they didn't just use their strength to break the rope and escape the camp. They easily could have done so, but they didn't even try.

He asked a trainer standing nearby. The trainer replied: 'When they're very young we use the same size rope to tie them up, and at that age it's enough to hold them. As they grow, they are conditioned to believe that they cannot break away. They believe the rope can still hold them, so they never try to escape.'

The only reason the elephants didn't try to break free was that they had adopted a belief over time that it just wasn't possible. So it is with people who spend day after day resisting something they wouldn't even want if they knew the truth. They continue to be addicts who don't use rather than becoming free people who have no desire to use. The poor elephants don't know any better, but as humans we can receive the truth as we grow on this journey that the rope cannot hold us any longer.

Why Willpower Doesn't Work

During the initial stages of recovery it may seem impossible that you could ever have no desire for the activity or substance, like a pipe dream that will always remain out of reach, and so a life of resisting it appears to be the only option. However, the clearer the trick becomes, the more the desire fades away and the more true freedom can prevail. Willpower to abstain is no longer needed, because we don't need willpower to abstain from eating vomit.

On the other hand, the thought of a lifelong battle of willpower resistance can sometimes seem appealing. How so? How can a worse option be more appealing? Well, on a certain level it creates a false sense of comfort. Some people have come to believe that it's safer to settle for accepted misery than to risk disappointment if it turns out something is too good to be true. Some are under the impression that the sense of pride they'll feel from fighting and winning a daily battle will balance out the sense of shame they've felt every time they lost that battle. Our loved ones often feed this idea of a constant battle because it helps them feel like they're being understanding, and it gives them some kind of consoling explanation when an addict keeps choosing the substance or compulsive behaviour over all that is good in their lives. But loved ones are also being tricked when they apply this thinking. Whole societies can be set free from the illusion!

One problem we have, however, is just how widespread the illusion is and just how successful the trick has been. I'm sure you've heard that it takes willpower to stay away from anything you have ever been addicted to. I'd be surprised if you'd never heard that, because it is the most common conclusion drawn by a population that has been tricked.

But more and more people are realising that it is a trick and breaking free from it.

One such person is the late smoking cessation expert, Allen Carr (not the comedian), who shed a lot of light on the concept of using willpower to quit something. Carr points out that willpower doesn't work because quitting involves a battle of wills.[15] We start off like the fly at the entrance to the pitcher plant, unaware of the impending danger. Then we start to bury our heads in the sand as our sense of control unravels. Next, something forces our heads out of the sand – such as our actions hurting someone, financial trouble, physical illness, terrible loss or anything notably bad being caused by the substance or activity of addiction – which gives us the desire to stop.

But the hijacked reward system compels us not to stop, and the tricked mind believes it is helping, even though logic says it can't be. Then, on top of that, our will to stop is diminished by horror stories from still-tricked people who are struggling daily and using willpower to abstain long term. Sometimes the will to stop is stronger because so-and-so happened or such-and-such matters more, but at other times the will to use is stronger because there's this celebration or that crisis and we feel deprived. One moment it makes sense to stop, so we will ourselves to stop, then another moment it makes sense to end the miserable resistance, so we will ourselves to use.

The stronger a person's willpower, the greater the battle. Sometimes the desire to use will outweigh the desire not to, and vice versa, hence the repeated attempts to stop and the repeated relapses. Ultimately, the will to use will be at internal war with the will to stop using for as long as the reward centre is hijacked. So while willpower has its benefits at certain times, it is not a logical, long-term quitting method, especially considering that constant battle creates 'decision fatigue' and leaves us preoccupied with saying no – keeping the mind focused on the very thing we're trying to resist. The stronger-willed someone is the stronger the willpower battle is, and the more miserable they'll be as they stop, relapse, stop, relapse, stop, relapse. Only the truth can truly set us free.

Can you relate to the elephant being held captive by something it had the power to break? What false beliefs have held you back?

....

....

....

....

Did you previously think that a life without addiction would mean a life of constant internal conflict? A life of resisting what you desperately want to have? How did that make you feel?

....

....

....

How do you feel when you consider the prospect of true freedom; a life in which you no longer want the substance or activity of your addiction? A life free from being hustled, from the Ponzi-scheming con artist, from the seducing psycho, from the pitcher plant, from the Munchausen by proxy sufferer, from the hijacker and from the faulty brain pathways? Free from the trick altogether?

....

....

....

....

....

Do you think you had weak willpower in the past or was it simply a strong battle of wills at play? Or both?

....

....

....

Choose Life!

Having said all this, an initial spurt of willpower is often essential when it comes to kick-starting the recovery journey. It's a temporary stepping stone, like training wheels on a bike or a stairgate for a child. We need it until the truth sinks to the point that we are no longer tempted. For many, willpower will be an essential part of the journey until the illusion melts away. Some people have a sudden epiphany or receive supernatural deliverance, but in other cases willpower will be required. Willpower to pick up this workbook, to go into rehab and to fight the all-encompassing desire until the desire is exposed as a trick. This initial willpower push-start is a tough valley of resistance most of us have to get through in order to make it to the high ground. It is usually during this difficult walk, during the craving period, that the heart of God (and my heart) cries out to you, over and over again, 'Oh, that you would choose life.'

In Deuteronomy, God tells the Israelites: 'Today I have given you the choice between life and death . . . Oh, that you would choose life . . .'[16]

Many times I have felt the depths of that 'oh'. It almost feels like an imploring or begging request. It's a championing effort. It goes beyond cheering on to success and stretches down to reach someone who is falling into failure. It's a yearning, a plea.

But no matter how strongly I have felt that 'oh' as I have looked into the eyes of someone tight-walking between life and death, it could never compare to how strongly God's heart is crying out to you right now, 'Oh, that you would choose life.'

Through the residential programme my husband and I run in the UK, most people who give up do so while they are fighting to resist what their hijacked brain is screaming for and their tricked mind is craving. Time after time someone will look me in the eye, often crying as they talk about how amazing our programme is, how much they love the staff and the friends they have made, how much they are learning and finding God, how they have never laughed so much or felt so loved, and how the house is the nicest place they've ever lived. Then they add that they have no idea why they are leaving, but they *are* leaving. This is agonising to witness, especially because the person hasn't yet experienced the joy and empowerment of a breakthrough, so they leave before they have found out that the ropes around their ankles can't actually hold them after all.

During this period of conscious self-restraint, it is essential to know that life doesn't have to stay that way; to know that the struggle is temporary and totally worth it; to know that the only direction from the bottom of the craving graph is up, and that the final destination is total freedom from craving, temptation and distorted desire.

It's essential to know that for yourself. Not just to read it in these pages and casually answer the questions, but to know it in a *gnōsesthe* way. To learn it, to experience it, to discuss it with God and with your supporter, to process it and to spend time really thinking about your answers to the questions. If you know deep down that you haven't been taking the truth in fully, feel free to go back to the start now, or you could do the whole of Part One twice. It matters far more that you *gnōsesthe* the truth than that you finish the course quickly. In fact, it's better to do Part One ten times and live in freedom for the rest of your life than to get it over with in a hurry and stay bound.

Healthy Boundaries

During this time of willpower-fuelled abstinence, you will need boundaries to keep you going. If you haven't already joined a residential programme or rehab, please give it some careful consideration. Not only will it provide the necessary temporary restrictions to your activities, but it should also offer support, prayer, counsel and provision for healing from trauma, as well as helping you learn life skills, and healthy coping mechanisms and perspectives – or even to unlearn unhealthy ones.

Falling

We had just sat down and started unpacking the picnic basket, ready to enjoy our food in front of an incredible view. It had taken some effort to get up the small mountain, but it was worth it for the spectacular vista.

All of a sudden he stood up, dazed, and walked towards the edge of the cliff. I assumed he wanted to explore the view before we ate, but he didn't stop walking. By the time I realised he wasn't going to stop at the edge, I jumped up and ran after him, but it was too late. I turned back to the path we had both walked up just moments earlier and ran to the bottom, calling for an ambulance on my way. When I got to the bottom he was sitting up and seemed surprisingly OK. It turned out the cliff edge wasn't a sheer drop, so the branches and ledges beneath had broken his fall. The ambulance arrived, patched up his cuts and warned that he might have concussion.

Before I could ask what had happened, he got up in a robotic fashion and made his way back up the mountain. I chased after him, but when we reached the top he just carried on walking and strode off the edge again! This time the paramedics were already there, but before they could deal with his broken bones he got up, walked back up and headed straight off the edge again. It was as if he were hypnotised! Every time he walked over the edge his mesmerised state intensified.

I screamed out for someone to help me restrain him – to force him into a car and drive him away from the mountain – but instead he was offered painkillers and padded clothing to make each fall less harmful. They said he was choosing to fall, and that he had a right to that choice so long as he didn't push anyone else off the edge.

I didn't know what to do. I needed to stop him falling just long enough to break the hypnosis. So I gathered everyone who would help and we built a brick wall around the edge of the cliff, high enough to stop him walking off it. Now I'm here with him every day, slowly breaking down the hypnotic state until, one day, we can remove the wall and enjoy the outstanding view together once again.

Addiction is like a hypnotic state that sends someone robotically over the edge of a cliff, time and time again. Each time the person goes over the cliff (by using the substance or activity of their addiction), it intensifies the hypnotic state.

It is at times like this that loved ones have to build a wall and create a restriction. Whether it's a residential programme or another environment, the rules and expectations put in place by loved ones can act as a temporary measure to prevent further harm and an increasingly hypnotic state. The more a person damages their reward centre through the use of substances and addictive behaviours, the more that person disappears and becomes replaced by an emptier, more robotic version of him or herself. It's the vicious cycle in which every use creates an increasing need for the next use.

The boundaries your loved ones put in place can help stop the vicious cycle just long enough for you to start breaking the hypnosis, to let the brain start healing and to let the truth sink in. But the goal should never be to leave the wall there permanently. Some people think the only solution to addiction is to build the wall as high as possible and then leave you to bump into it forever, just to stop you dying from the next fall or a future fall. If that's the plan, people find themselves having to build the wall higher and higher and higher.

The Law of Sin and Death

It's important to use any walls necessary while you learn more about the trick your addiction is playing, but just being 'clean and dry' without really knowing the truth – while still believing that the substance or activity has something to offer you, and that you still want it but can't let yourself have it – you will continue to be an addict who isn't using. On the other hand, fighting tooth and nail to avoid using so you can be of sober mind to learn the truth that sets you free, that's what God has invested in for you. Even people who don't know God can get free from addiction, but they cannot get free from the root issue: the law of sin and death.

Your brain healing has to coincide with a psychological realisation that the whole desire for the drug was a sick and twisted illusion. Yes, there's often a physical withdrawal, but we all know this isn't the real battle. We'd suffer flu-like symptoms for two weeks any day if it resulted in us getting free forever. It's the hijacked brain that's the real problem. The period of agonising, willpower-fuelled determination against desire is like childbirth. It's the unavoidable, painful phase required to bring forth new life, but thankfully it's not a permanent state of being!

At our residential programme, we sometimes say, 'The two and three will get you through the first few weeks.' This refers to a temptation scale I was inspired to create, which we often use. We'll discuss it in more detail later, but for now I'll share it below so you can think about where you are on the scale (almost everyone starts at the very beginning):

Temptation Scale

1. I really, *really* want it! It's taking everything I have to stop myself from using.

2. I want it, but I don't want the consequences.

3. I want it, but I love [insert anything you risk losing or causing harm to by using] too much.

4. I want it, but I don't *want* to want it any more.

5. I'm starting not to want it.

6. My feelings and thoughts are telling me I want it, but I understand that it's just my old brain pathways. If I remember that, I realise I don't actually want it at all.

7. I sometimes have the odd feeling or thought from the old pathways, but I know straightaway that I don't actually want it.

8. I don't really have any desire for it any more, but I'm aware of other things that could pull me back, such as [insert low self-worth, imposter syndrome, self-sabotage, unforgiveness, resentment, the effects of unresolved trauma, the name of a person or parent, or whatever it is that is still impacting you].

9. I want it so little that even calling it a temptation feels odd these days.

10. I'm not even slightly tempted by that substance or activity any more. In fact, I hate what it does to people. I'd rather eat my own vomit than fall for it again!

Finding True Freedom

People often say that you shouldn't start your recovery if you're doing it for someone else, and there are good reasons why people might think that. But if your recovery includes discovering the truth and breaking free from the illusion, points two and three on the temptation scale – avoiding negative circumstances and doing it for your loved ones – can act as a wall around the cliff edge. This can give you the initial determination you need to resist the strongest desires while the hypnosis is broken and the truth is learned. However, resisting the desire rarely works as a long-term solution, regardless of the motivation. Because even if it stops you walking off the cliff edge, it won't make you free.

Resisting the desire forever is not true freedom. True freedom is losing the desire altogether because you see the witches for what they are, because the hypnotism has worn off, because the brain has healed and the mind has broken free of the trick. Resisting the desire to use is only worthwhile as a means to freedom. You can rely on willpower long enough to let the brain heal and learn the truth; until you have lost the desire for the thing you only ever desired because your brain was hijacked.

Living the rest of your life as someone who wants something but abstains from it because other things matter more is not a pleasant prospect. Sure, it'll give you a sense of pride, which feels good after years of shame, and thinking of it as an incurable disease gives loved ones a reason to stop blaming you and makes others feel protected from it happening to them, but it's still a prison sentence. An addict refusing to use the activity or substance they think they want is still an addict. Not only does God want a better life for you than that – not only did Jesus die so you could have freedom from it – but living like that simply doesn't make sense when you look at how addiction works.

The initial phases of recovery, withdrawal and abstinence are not the only times God will implore you, 'Oh, that you would choose life.' This will be a strong topic for further resources because it is essential to your ongoing success. If you are already beyond the point of withdrawal and craving, yet you still find yourself walking the tightrope between life and death, addiction and freedom, don't worry. You're not alone, and there will be more answers for you as you continue with this course.

What has stood out most to you so far?

....

....

....

....

....

Have you ever tried to pursue abstinence through willpower as a long-term plan? How did it go?

....

....

....

How different does the idea of abstinence seem when you know that it's just a temporary phase on the way to a life of complete freedom?

....

....

....

Try to imagine reaching point ten on the temptation scale, where you have zero desire for the substance or activity. It might be hard to believe you will ever get there if you've spent years being duped, but try really hard to imagine it. How does it feel?

....

....

....

What will you remember in an attempt to stop yourself walking off the cliff edge on your most difficult days?

....

....

....

Dear God . . .

(For those who are not Christians)

. . . I'm staying open-minded – and open-hearted.

If you're hearing these prayers, thank you. I pray that one day I'll hear you back.

(For anyone)

. . . You are God, I am not. What a relief!

But you are a God who put on skin and came into our human experience – who suffered and hurt and was tempted – so you know how it feels.

Thank you for this course. Thank you for everything I'm learning and realising. Thank you that there's so much more to come, and that I'm going from strength to strength just by still being here.

I confess that this is hard right now, and sometimes I feel fearful, sad and lost. But I know that truth is higher than feeling.

Please help me persevere through the tough bits so I can discover and enjoy the good bits. Please help me discover more of you through the difficult points and the easy points.

Amen

You've achieved Milestone Four!

Statement of truth:

I will be free from all wrong desire once I have truly understood that addiction is a trick and know how it works. In the meantime, I will exercise willpower as a temporary means.

'Then you will know the truth, and the truth will set you free'

John 8:32

Milestone Five:

Allowing Pain to Work
In Your Favour

'Then you will know the
truth, and the truth
will set you free.'

John 8:32

Pain

Pain is part of life for everyone, everywhere on earth: from broken bones to broken families; from malignant cells to malignant behaviour in relationships. But addiction and pain are innately intertwined. Addictive substances and activities deceitfully offer to soothe our pain while cunningly creating it. As a result, cutting off the addiction rapidly exposes us to pain. This inevitably leads to a confused psychology of pain in any addict.

Have you ever looked at the non-addicts in your life and wondered how they manage to cope better with a horrific loss than you do with a headache? Me too! I noticed that difference while my brain was hijacked. It made me feel so rubbish about myself, as if they were strong people and I wasn't. Or maybe you tell yourself they've never been damaged the way you have – even though that's not always true.

The truth is, you're not weaker or irrevocably damaged, you're addicted to something. The addiction has made you incapable of dealing with difficulty, healing from trauma or mending your broken heart. It has tricked you into thinking that it's helping you deal with things, but look at the non-addicts around you who have been sick, abused, abandoned, neglected, traumatised or bereaved. They have been hurt, but they have also healed. They were broken but they found restoration. Now think about the addicts around you. Do any of them cope well with the challenges of life? Have they healed from trauma, grief, internal struggle or sickness?

Someone who is in pain but isn't addicted may go through agony. But they eventually heal. Someone who is traumatised and addicted will experience momentary relief from the pain, but the pain will be prolonged by the substance or activity, which adds more trauma on top of it. The pain will never heal while they're addicted. Even if an addict never experienced trauma before they became an addict, the wound, discomfort, emptiness or unfulfilled need that was originally there has gone unsolved and been prolonged, and things have got much worse since then. It's incredible how even using food to pacify stress or discomfort prolongs the problem.

Your brain was not hijacked because you are innately weaker than other people. You are not more pathetic as a person. You are not damaged beyond repair. You are addicted. It is the addiction that makes you incapable of coping or healing. Without the addiction you would regain the inner strength required to cope and heal. In time, when your brain damage has healed and your soul has been freed by the truth, you will begin to heal and cope with things. And as a result of the truth that has been revealed, you will likely cope with pain better than you did before addiction and better than many non-addicts do.

To get to that point, however, you must break free from the trick, reverse the hijacking, and relearn some of things addiction has wrongly taught you – not least about pain. Addiction teaches us false things about pain until we perceive it completely differently from the way people whose brains haven't been hijacked do. This is even evident in the way addicts pop painkillers at the slightest twinge (especially when they're not using) or fall apart over something that non-addicts would ride like an unexpected wave. Again, these things don't happen because we are unusually weak, but because that's what addiction does. However, it can be undone.

Have you ever judged yourself as weak compared to people who cope better with pain than you? Do you avoid people who make you feel that way? Or tell yourself that your pain is worse than theirs? Or have you done all of the above? If so, how?

....

....

....

....

List some of the differences in the way addicts deal with pain compared with non-addicts.

....

....

....

....

....

....

....

....

Can you think of a recent example of pain you went through that you would have dealt with better if your brain hadn't been hijacked? How might you have coped differently without the addiction?

....

....

....

....

Can you think of one or two people you've looked up to or wondered how they cope so well with things? What is different about the way they cope compared with you?

....

....

....

....

List the most prominent pains you experienced before addiction that the substance / activity did not resolve or heal?

....

....

....

....

....

List the most prominent pains in your life that your addiction has caused.

....

....

....

The Eleventh-Day

Pain is resistance. It pushes against us, and addicts naturally resist resistance. But what if the resistance of pain could work in our favour?

Just before the UK's Covid-19 lockdown, I signed up for a personal trainer at the gym because I had been in a fitness rut for a while and knew I needed a good kick to get me out of it. His name was Andy, and he really helped me out of that rut and back into the flow. But he also made me realise something about strength and resistance. I had exercised a lot over the years, but I had always pushed myself with exertion rather than resistance. I had never before pushed it to the point where the pain of one more rep made me feel like my limbs might fall off.

One day I was doing bicep curls. I found the first eight reps surprisingly easy, but the ninth was a strain. Then suddenly the tenth was really difficult, and the eleventh was so difficult that halfway through I didn't think I would be able to finish it. The pain was so intense and my arms just didn't feel strong enough.

In that moment, as I was literally growling, Andy said something profound. 'The eleventh one is the one that matters. The resistance is what creates the strength. The other ten were a waste without this one.'

With that, I completed the eleventh curl and dropped the weights.

Wow! Without the eleventh rep, the previous ten would have been pointless. When you begin this journey of recovery, you will hit a lot of 'eleventh-days'; days when it feels like you can't finish. But this is the day that all the previous ones were there to get us to. The 'eleventh-day' is the day that matters. It can come any day, it can come a few times on different days, but it's an 'eleventh-day' to you.

When that dopamine is in deficit and the ingrained pathways are doing what they've been trained to do, it hurts. It's sheer resistance. It's your 'eleventh-day'. You may not believe you can finish it. You may not think you are strong enough. But it is the days when we feel that way that count the most!

When it comes to fitness, resistance causes muscle atrophy, a process of tearing and repairing that builds stronger muscle. So it is with our souls. Too often we resist the resistance, thinking that the tearing is a reason to stop, that the pain is a sign to give up. But actually, it's the tearing that leads to strength.

'I'm just not strong enough.'

We've all heard those words. And we've probably spoken them, too, or at least thought them. But the reality is, the only way to *get* strong enough is to finish the eleven.

Within weeks of that first day with Andy, I needed double the weight to get the same level of resistance because I was so much stronger. I loved the feeling of climbing up the ranks of those dumbbells, kettlebells and discs, going from strength to strength. Months later, when I used the same weight as I had that first day, I bicep-curled about twenty-five reps before I got too bored to carry on. I found no resistance in that weight any more!

The same is true when it comes to your recovery. The weight that is giving you so much resistance today will one day feel light. The resistance of the 'eleventh-days' will one day feel like nothing.

How do you normally respond to resistance, when you don't feel like you can do it any more?

....

....

....

What practical methods can you put in place to help you finish the 'eleventh rep' every time?

....

....

....

Ignoring the Pain Makes It Worse

We tend to see pain as something that can only be bad – something to resist or escape from – but it has its uses. It builds us up to be stronger, but it also acts as a sign.

Engine Alert

'Are you sure, Clyde?' It was a rhetorical question. Not one bit of me believed that my husband was sure.

'Yeah,' he answered, full of casual confidence, 'it's fine! These dashboard lights always come on early, just to give you a warning. I know my car. We're fine.'

'Early? That engine light's been flashing for ages, and now the car's making that noise.' His nonchalant optimism had done nothing to reassure me. 'It's really worrying me now.'

'Stop looking at it, then,' he said, leaning forward and using his hand to momentarily hide the dashboard warning light.

'That won't make the problem go away. I don't understand why you didn't have the engine checked at the garage just now.'

'Because we're late.'

'But we'll be even later if we break down!'

'We won't break—'

With that, a huge thud made us jump out of our seats and we yelled out loud as Clyde swerved out of the middle lane towards the hard shoulder. Even though it made no sense, we were both convinced that the engine had literally fallen through the bottom of the car onto the motorway. That's what it sounded like.

Having just made it to safety, we jumped out, shaken, and ran up the embankment to catch our breath.

Guess what? We were late to our appointment that day. *Very* late.

Pain is often like the engine light on my husband's dashboard, trying to alert us to something that needs our attention. We only feel pain because humanity decided to stray from God, yet in his grace he has made our pain useful. God lets our consequential pain act as a warning light, alerting us to fix a deeper problem.

Most of us don't like pain. It feels bad, and sometimes it seems as though resolving it properly will get in the way of other things, as my husband did with the car engine. He didn't think we had time to stop and fix the problem to which the dashboard light was alerting us. We were on our way somewhere, and it was an inconvenience. But the consequence of ignoring it was far worse than the process of dealing with it properly in the first place.

When it comes to pain, people often try to do what Clyde suggested we do in that car – ignore it. Other times we actively cover it up, as he tried to do with his hand. It amazes me how often, and how strongly, we are encouraged to cover up our pain. It goes without saying that there is big profit in pain relief. Companies, groups and individuals cultivate the flawed temptation we feel to ignore or cover up our pain rather than fixing the root cause. They make money from it – unimaginable amounts of money sometimes. Their only concern with regard to the breakdown that inevitably follows is the hope that we'll spend more money to escape it.

From taking painkillers for a headache instead of drinking enough water or discovering a tumour that needs to be removed, to taking drugs to fix heartache instead of turning to God or finding an emotional tumour to remove; from oxy to heroin, from fast food to alcohol, from porn to the races – all of these 'solutions' offer us a chance to disconnect the engine light... and they all make money for someone in the process. Lots of money. But worst of all, our spiritual enemy (who we'll learn more about soon) gets his fill because preventing us from dealing with our problem keeps us bound and away from God.

As horrible as pain is, it can also be useful. Covering it up may be good for a toxic economy, but it's extremely bad for us. It can leave us physically or emotionally stranded on a motorway embankment with a written-off car! And ignoring it only makes it worse.

I remember when I broke my foot and carried on hobbling, driving and even passionately pacing as I preached on it. When I finally went to hospital six days later, the doctor gave me a good telling off and said that the delay had extended the pain and length of my recovery. We do the same thing when we put off our recovery from addiction.

Can you think of any pain you have suffered because someone else ignored or covered up their own pain? What happened?

....

....

....

....

....

....

....

Is there any pain in your own life that could cause you and / or someone else further pain if you covered it up? How would that look? What would happen if you were to deal with the pain instead?

....

....

....

....

....

....

Give three examples of pain you are feeling now, or have recently felt, and the problems these pains may have been alerting you to deal with before they got worse.

....

....

....

....

....

Can you think of any logical reason to delay your recovery when you know that doing so will make the process harder and longer when you do face it?

....

....

....

There was a popular television show in the UK called *One Born Every Minute*. Each episode focuses on two or three labour ward patients and allows viewers to witness everything they go through. Some of the women had easier labours than others. I remember one episode in which a mother in a birthing pool told the midwife the baby was coming, and before the midwife made it to the door to ask for assistance the baby was out! But some went through such agony that they repeatedly declared they couldn't do it, and that they wanted it to stop.

I have often wondered, what if a woman in labour could stop? What if she could just change her mind, refuse to continue the process and decide that the baby wasn't worth the pain or that it was just too hard, regardless of the child's value? What if she could just quit? It's painful, so why not? The reality is that this pain precedes new life. For some people in recovery the pain is relatively easy, but for others it is such agony that they repeatedly declare that they cannot do it and they want to stop. Sadly, unlike women in child labour, addicts in recovery *can* choose to stop. They can just change their minds, give up and walk away. But it is one of the saddest things on earth when they do, because they were so close to that new life and all of its joy. So close to saying, 'It was so worth it.' So close to seeing that the pain was just a passageway to new life.

Putting the Pieces Back Together

Have you ever seen a medical drama or documentary in which an open fracture is realigned? Maybe you've even experienced it first hand. It's not pretty! But it reveals a powerful principle that relates strongly to the pain we go through during recovery. When someone presents with an open fracture, their bone has snapped into two or more pieces, and one piece has torn through the skin. They are in a lot of pain. Their body is severely damaged and deformed, and they are losing blood.

I've never had an open fracture, but one thing struck me both times I saw TV medics deal with this injury in crisis contexts without any anaesthetic to hand. Each time the patient screamed more as the bone was realigned than they did when it was left in pieces. As the medic holds the patient's foot or hand and forcefully yanks it out and back in with skilled precision, the pain of that realignment far exceeds the pain of the injury itself. Do you see? The process of healing initially hurts more than the brokenness.

And the pain doesn't just go away after that. I even saw one case in which the doctor was unsuccessful the first time because the patient fought him, and he had to realign it twice! The horrendous pain is worth it for the subsequent healing, but it's also worth remembering that the alternative is ongoing blood loss and infection. Imagine if someone with an open fracture dragged herself out of an army medical tent, declaring that the realignment was too painful and she was better off on her own with a bit of morphine while she figured out a different solution. The bone would become more deformed, the torn skin would get infected and the body would continue to lose blood. That wound would become septic in no time! And the woman with the fracture would grow weaker and weaker with every drop of blood loss.

Fracture, pierced skin and blood loss is what we go through as addicts. The initial break often happens before the addiction takes over. Therefore, we enter recovery in pieces, torn and running on empty. But as awful as it is to be in that state, the realignment of recovery can hurt so much more. The pulling back of the hand or foot is like the nightmares, the recurring memories, the full thrust of unnumbed emotions, the realisation of what you've done and what others have done to you, the anger, the despair, the anguish, the overwhelm.

And even when the 'limb' falls back into place, it doesn't all suddenly disappear. Some people need to go through the yanking process a second time, or perhaps more times if they keep fighting it. After that comes the ongoing rehabilitation of the limb, as the injury has affected the entire body. The ache of bones fusing back together, the sting of stitched-up skin, the throbbing all over as the person has to learn how to use the damaged arm or leg again.

Recovery from addiction often hurts more than the addiction itself. But addiction prolongs pain, whereas recovery heals pain.

Can you think any good things that can come out of pain, such as the pain experienced in childbirth?

....

....

....

....

Can you think of any times in your life when pain led to something positive? If not, can you think of a time in your life when pain could have led to something positive if you had persevered through it?

....

....

....

....

If someone you love was in a car accident and refused treatment because the treatment hurt more than the injuries, what would you say to them?

....

....

....

....

What could you stick on a Post-it note by your bed or on your mirror for the days when the pain of recovery is at its worst?

....

....

....

....

Dear God . . .

(For those who are not Christians)

. . . If you care about my pain and are able to heal me, I want that. But if I decide to follow you, it will be because I have discovered that you are worthy to be followed, regardless of what you can do for me. Because you are a good God who chooses to do good things.

(For anyone)

. . . You are God, I am not. What a relief!

You are familiar with my pain. You have been present through it all, willing me to let you help.

Thank you for going through the greatest pain anyone has ever felt to open up the way to eternal life and healing. Thank you that the pain hasn't killed me and that it won't kill me now, because you are taking me through healing – not destructive – pain.

I confess that I spent too long ignoring and covering up my pain, that I prolonged it by avoiding the real problem. Please help me persevere through any pain that is essential to healing. I pray that I will one day be the person who helps someone else persevere through their healing pain.

Amen

You've achieved Milestone Five!

Statement of truth:

I accept that some pain is useful, some pain is necessary and some pain brings healing. I determine to let pain do its job in my recovery and life.

'Then you will know the truth, and the truth will set you free'

John 8:32

Twelve Statements of Truth

1. I realise and accept that my choices, behaviour and feelings have been influenced by a con, and that I can break free from it by knowing and understanding how the con works.

2. I realise that addiction is a type of brain damage, but that God gave my brain the ability to heal when his amazing design is hijacked.

3. I recognise that a craving is the feeling caused by faulty brain activity, and a vicious cycle in which every use makes me need the next use. I understand that using continues the craving, while not using stops it.

4. I will be free from all wrong desire once I have truly understood that addiction is a trick and know how it works. In the meantime, I will exercise willpower as a temporary means.

5. I accept that some pain is useful, some pain is necessary and some pain brings healing. I determine to let pain do its job in my recovery and life.

6. I recognise that an enemy provides false relief, but God sacrificed himself to provide true freedom.

7. I accept and appreciate the struggles and joys of process for all the good it can produce in me.

8. I refuse to settle for anything less than true transformation.

9. I choose to increasingly believe what is true about myself and reject the lies.

10. I recognise God's holiness and my sin. I choose to approach God in repentance, which I can only do because Jesus made a way for me to become pure through his own sacrifice. I recognise that God loves me, so I don't need to live in shame but can continue to be sanctified by his Holy Spirit, who lives in me.

11. I consciously decide to forgive the wrongs committed against me, and I accept God's forgiveness for all the wrongs I have done.

12. I seek to make amends where I am responsible and put things right where possible, in the full confidence that Jesus has righted my wrongs spiritually and eternally, and will one day right all wrongs.

Endnotes

Milestone One

1. Mimi Davis, 'Greek Words for "Know" in the New Testament': https://sweeterthanhoneyministry.com/2016/02/25/greek-words-for-know-in-the-new-testament (accessed 9 July 2022). (*Gnōsesthe* is a derivative of the word *ginosko*).

2. Wycliffe Bible Translators, 'Latest Bible translation statistics': https://www.wycliffe.org.uk/about/our-impact (accessed 7 July 2022).

3. Will van der Hart and Rob Waller, *The Perfectionism Book* (IVP: 2016), p. 93.

Milestone Two

4. Romans 7:15.

5. Inspire Malibu: https://www.inspiremalibu.com/blog/alcohol-addiction/understanding-addiction-reward-and-pleasure-in-the-brain (accessed 7 June 2022); Heads Up, 'Recovery From Drug Addiction': http://headsup.scholastic.com/students/recovery-from-drug-addiction (accessed 7 June 2022).

6. Caroline Leaf, *Who Switched Off my Brain?* (Thomas Nelson: 2009), p. 15.

7. Steve Goss and Mary Wren, *Keys to Health, Wholeness & Fruitfulness* (Freedom in Christ Ministries International: 2019), pp. 51–2.

8. Proverbs 23:7.

9. Philippians 4:8.

10. Matthew 6:24.

11. University of Vienna, 'Objectification of women results in lack of empathy': https://www.yourbrainonporn.com/relevant-research-and-articles-about-the-studies/porn-use-sex-addiction-studies/objectification-of-women-results-in-lack-of-empathy-2018/ Cortex Study (accessed 7 June 2022).

12. James Clear, 'How Vietnam War Veterans Broke Their Heroin Addictions': https://jamesclear.com/heroin-habits (accessed 7 June 22).

13. National Institutes of Health, 'Drugs, Brains, and Behavior: The Science of Addiction Treatment and Recovery': https://www.drugabuse.gov/publications/drugs-brains-behavior-science-addiction/treatment-recovery; Heads Up, 'Recovery From Drug Addiction': https://headsup.scholastic.com/students/recovery-from-drug-addiction (both accessed 7 June 2022).

Milestone Three

14. Allen Carr, *Allen Carr's Easy Way to Stop Smoking* (Penguin Books: 2015), pp. 48-49) and Neil T. Anderson's *Overcoming Addictive Behaviour* (Bethany House: 2003), p. 30.

Milestone Four

15. https://dictionary.cambridge.org/dictionary/english/abstain.

16. https://www.lexico.com/definition/abstain.

17. https://www.merriam-webster.com/dictionary/willpower.

18. Allen Carr, *Allen Carr's Easy Way To Stop Smoking* (Penguin Books: 2015 pp. 94–103).

19. Deuteronomy 30:19, (NLT).